Designing Data-Intensive Applications

2 books in 1 - The Ultimate Framework to Building, Scaling, and Optimizing Reliable Data Systems. From Fundamentals to Real-World Mastery

By
Mark Reed & Cyberedge Press

Table of Contents

Designing Data Intensive Applications

BOOK 1

Introduction

W e're living in a data-driven world. One where we interact with data in a vast array of functions. This wide range of functions covers online ticket bookings, social media sites, and augmented reality games that convert real-world objects into points on a scoreboard. The people who manage these sites know that for them, data is more than an asset; it's the very lifeblood of innovation. These sites are dependent on quality data to enable them to provide basic services to users.

These services rely on algorithms to help them manipulate the data they work with. The algorithms work to curate your social media feeds, suggest your next favorite movie, and use financial models to predict stock prices. What they have in common is that they all hinge on the successful manipulation of data.

In today's fast-paced technology landscape, the relevance of data-driven applications has skyrocketed. Major industries—from healthcare to entertainment—rely heavily on the effective management and utilization of data. The healthcare industry stores patient records that include their identification details, medical diagnoses, and various medications that have been prescribed for different illnesses. The entertainment industry uses what they know about viewer preferences to keep them entertained with an endless stream of viewing suggestions that appeal to each individual viewer.

This book will help you harness the power of data through the use of Python. In it, you will find out how to set up the Python development environment and its libraries. Every step you take through this book will bring you closer to mastering the art of designing and optimizing data-intensive applications using Python.

Python's simplicity and readability enable rapid development and versatility across diverse applications. It uses libraries and frameworks like Pandas, Apache Kafka, SQLAchemy, and PySpark to access distributed data, making it a preferred choice for beginners and professionals alike. Its libraries provide pre-built functions and tools that streamline the development process, enhance productivity, and allow developers to leverage existing solutions rather than building from scratch.

These are the tools and techniques that ensure data flows smoothly at breakneck speeds, enabling timely decisions and groundbreaking innovations. Without a clear grasp of these advanced concepts, even the most talented coders can find themselves lagging behind in the race for technological progress.

This book aims to help you bridge the gap between basic coding skills and the intricate art of designing and optimizing data-intensive applications. If you're a software developer or a data engineer looking to escalate your knowledge, you've picked up the right guide.

The instructions you receive here will inform you how to create scalable data-intensive applications to effectively access, manipulate, and leverage big data.

The book goes beyond simply explaining these complex ideas. It offers practical, hands-on projects that mirror the real-world challenges that you'll face in the industry. Whether it's building scalable data pipelines or optimizing distributed systems, you won't just read about these concepts—you'll implement them.

The understanding that you will gain in advanced concepts in data engineering is not just beneficial; it's crucial. To benefit your learning journey, this book will cover distributed systems architecture, manipulating and optimizing data systems, common algorithms used in data applications, and advanced topics such as microservices and RESTful APIs.

Mastery of these areas means differentiating yourself in a saturated field. Distributed systems, real-time data processing, and efficient data pipelines are not buzzwords—they're essential components of modern data engineering.

The detailed instructions in this book are suitable for mid-level developers. If you are new to the field, you will benefit from the explanations provided. However, you may need to augment your knowledge if you want to follow the coding instructions.

For those with more than a foundational understanding of programming, the challenge now is not just to keep up but to lead. You will gain practical experience by working on case studies rooted in actual industry problems, breaking them down step-by-step, and then solving them using the techniques you've learned. This hands-on approach ensures you can directly apply your newfound skills to tackle complex issues seamlessly.

Understanding the core principles will lay a strong foundation upon which to build more complex structures. As you progress, each project and case study will serve as a crucial milestone, marking your advancement from a capable coder to an expert data engineer.

You'll find yourself better equipped to handle the demands of a rapidly evolving tech landscape where data reigns supreme. Without data, services like airline ticketing, social media, and financial analysis sites would have no information with which to engage users. More importantly, you'll gain a deeper appreciation of how integral data engineering is to the broader spectrum of technology and innovation.

The goal is to make you proficient in handling large-scale data applications and comfortable with leveraging modern techniques and tools to simplify complex tasks.

Your ability to solve industry challenges will set you apart, positioning you as a leader in data engineering. Together, we'll explore the intricacies of data engineering, confront real-world challenges, and develop the expertise that will make you indispensable in any data-focused role. So, whether you're here to deepen your understanding, enhance your professional skills, or gear up for an interview, this journey will transform how you think about and work with data.

As you turn each page, you're preparing not just for day-to-day tasks but also for critical career moments like system design interviews. With the tech industry being so fiercely competitive when it comes to roles centered around data, you will benefit from the skills that you acquire here. They will open new doors, presenting opportunities to innovate within your current role or even land that dream job you've been eyeing.

Job seekers aiming for data engineering positions face rigorous interviews that test not only their technical abilities but also their problem-solving acumen and innovative thinking. Through the comprehensive coverage of key concepts, this book will arm you with the knowledge and confidence to excel in those high-stakes scenarios.

By the final chapter, you'll have a solid grasp of complex data engineering skills. You'll also be more than prepared to face system design interviews with confidence as you will be equipped with a toolkit of modern technologies and methodologies.

Are you prepared to navigate the exciting, complex world of data-intensive applications with Python as your guide? If so, turn to the first chapter and let the adventure begin.

CHAPTER 1

Introduction to Data-Intensive Applications

D ata-intensive applications require frequent changes in data. This can present unique challenges and opportunities. CPU-intensive systems were the predecessor of data-intensive applications. While the previous method emphasized computational performance, the new approach focuses on managing large volumes of data efficiently while maintaining data integrity. To develop robust and scalable solutions capable of handling complex data tasks, it is important to grasp the principles that govern data-intensive applications. This chapter introduces the foundational concepts necessary for achieving this goal, thus setting the stage for effective system design and implementation.

We will explore the distinguishing characteristics of data-intensive applications, including their:

- scalability

- reliability

- fault tolerance

This chapter outlines core concepts in data engineering. It focuses on:

- data modeling

- storage technologies

- best practices in data lifecycle management

- techniques for maintaining data quality

- how to maintain data consistency

These are crucial for structuring and managing large datasets. By examining real-world examples and exploring different approaches to scalability, readers will gain a comprehensive understanding of how to design applications that can efficiently handle large-scale data processing tasks.

Understanding Data-Intensive vs. CPU-Intensive Systems

Understanding the distinctions between data-intensive and CPU-intensive systems will lay the groundwork for developing robust, scalable, and reliable data systems.

Data-intensive applications are primarily concerned with the efficient management of data.

While CPU-intensive systems focus on maximizing computational performance, data-intensive systems are focused on efficiently handling large volumes of complex data. These systems store, retrieve, and process this data, often across multiple servers.

Consider an e-commerce platform with millions of transactions per day. Here, the challenge lies not in performing calculations swiftly but in managing, querying, and storing enormous datasets efficiently. Similarly, streaming services like Netflix prioritize data handling capacity to offer a seamless user experience. The volume and diversity of data in such cases often matter more than the speed at which raw computations are performed.

Scalability

One of the defining characteristics of data-intensive applications is scalability. This refers to the growth that these systems must accommodate. Growth can be in the form of data volume, user base, or application features. Accommodating a growing database needs to be done without compromising performance. There are two ways that systems can scale:

1. **Vertical scaling,** which involves adding more power to existing servers

2. **Horizontal scaling,** which entails adding more servers to distribute the load of work that each server has to carry

Reliability

Reliability ensures that the system remains operational even in challenging conditions. To enable reliability, various measures can be implemented, such as redundancy and failover mechanisms. This requires implementing backup components so that they can take over when the main servers and components fail. Doing this will increase the system's capacity for fault tolerance, allowing it to continue functioning correctly even when parts of it malfunction.

Accuracy

Data consistency and integrity refer to the need for data to remain accurate and consistent across multiple server instances. Having data that is the same across all servers that are accessed for your services is vital for preventing errors and inconsistencies.

Financial institutions are examples of institutions that must maintain transaction accuracy and integrity to avoid severe consequences.

ACID Technique

Techniques like ACID (atomicity, consistency, isolation, durability) properties in databases ensure that transactions are processed reliably, maintaining data integrity.

The use of the ACID technique consists of:

- **Atomicity**: This refers to the monitoring of each transaction to determine whether it has been successful. Successful transactions are committed while unsuccessful transactions are aborted.

- **Consistency**: The data remains consistent and correct before the time of the transaction. Once the transaction is committed, the state of the data is consistent with the newly-committed updates.

- **Isolation**: Each transaction is performed in isolation from other transactions. The data for these transactions is isolated from the rest of the data throughout the change process. Once the change has been committed, the data is then reconciled with the greater data pool.

- **Durability**: All committed changes are permanent.

This process is applied in ride-sharing apps like Uber, which require real-time data consistency to effectively match drivers with passengers.

CPU-Intensive

Rather than managing massive amounts of data, CPU-intensive systems focus on efficiently performing heavy computations.

These systems excel at tasks involving extensive mathematical modeling, simulations, or complex algorithmic computations. Practical applications can be found in the areas of:

- scientific computing applications used for climate modeling

- genetic sequencing

- financial risk assessment models

Performance metrics in CPU-intensive systems often revolve around the efficiency of the computation itself, measured in terms:

- processing speed

- throughput

- latency

Data-Intensive Applications in the Real-World

Let us look at some real-world examples to help illuminate the different needs for data-intensive versus CPU-intensive systems.

Firms like Google and Facebook are prime examples of organizations that operate data-intensive systems.

- **Google's** search engine requires it to document the location of huge amounts of data. Its email and other productivity services require the storage and retrieval of large amounts of individual users at any given time.

- **Facebook**, on the other hand, needs to offer its users individualized content that includes friends' stories, product suggestions, and event updates.

The primary concern of these and many other web-based organizations is to handle and analyze petabytes of data generated every minute from user interactions, advertisements, and content uploads. On the other hand, organizations involved in high-frequency trading rely on CPU-intensive systems to execute complex algorithms within milliseconds to capitalize on market opportunities. The systems that require CPU-intensive operations are dependent on speed of execution rather than access to a large amount of data. Can you think of any organizations where time has been of the essence when waiting for a response? In situations where a delayed response can cause a user to lose an opportunity, It is likely that the system was more CPU-intensive than data-intensive.

Choosing the wrong system design can have significant implications. Developing a data-intensive application using principles suited for CPU-intensive systems could lead to inefficiencies, bottlenecks, and scalability issues. This would be due to the inability of the system to efficiently work with large quantities of data. CPU-intensive systems tend to store their data locally, making for faster computations. Conversely, data-intensive systems require access to data that may be stored at various locations. Rather than compute this data, data-intensive systems collate it in meaningful ways and then present it to the user.

A CPU-intensive system is limited in its ability to scale to a level similar to that of a data-intensive application. This is due to the restrictions it faces when it comes to storing and working with data elements. Conversely, applying data-centric approaches to CPU-intensive tasks may result in underutilized computational resources and slower performance.

For instance, a healthcare analytics platform built with an emphasis on computational power might struggle with data storage and retrieval, impeding its ability to provide timely insights. This is because doctors and pharmacists need to access patient data from various locations to help them make decisions. Their need to make calculations is low, while their dependence on information is high.

This healthcare example illustrates to us how making informed decisions in system design is dependent on the specific requirements of the application being built. If your project involves handling large-scale data processing, look for solutions that prioritize data management, storage optimization, and efficient querying. For instance, utilizing distributed databases like Cassandra or HBase can ensure your system handles horizontal scaling effectively.

Conversely, if your application is numbers-based and requires heavy computational processes, optimizing your system for rapid calculations through parallel processing techniques and high-performance computing clusters will be necessary.

Core Concepts in Data Engineering

Understanding core data engineering concepts is paramount in the world of data-intensive applications. This foundational knowledge aids in designing systems that are efficient, scalable, and reliable. Here, we explore key concepts, including Data Modeling, Data Storage Technologies, Data Lifecycle Management, and Data Quality and Consistency.

Data Modeling

Data modeling forms the bedrock of any data-intensive application. At its core, data modeling involves structuring data according to relationships and rules. This process begins with schema design, which defines how data is organized in databases and data warehouses. A well-designed schema simplifies data access and analysis, making it easy to query and retrieve necessary information.

Schemas

Schemas can be categorized into normalization and denormalization techniques.

Normalization

Normalization involves organizing data to reduce redundancy and improve data integrity by dividing large tables into smaller, related ones. This technique follows specific rules, usually called normal forms. These norms ensure that each table contains only data related to a single entity or concept. For instance, in an e-commerce database, customer information might be kept separate from order details to avoid duplicating customer information storage every time an order is placed.

Denormalization

Conversely, denormalization merges data to improve read performance at the cost of some redundancy. This approach might be used when quick data retrieval is essential, such as in data warehousing used by CPU-intensive applications where analytical queries are common. These contrasting techniques highlight the importance of balancing data integrity and query performance based on specific use cases.

Data Storage Technologies

Choosing appropriate data storage technologies is crucial for managing the vast amounts of data handled by modern applications. The primary options include SQL and NoSQL databases, each with unique implications for data management.

SQL Databases

SQL databases, also known as relational databases, use structured schemas defining tables, columns, and their relationships. These kinds of databases are favorable for CPU-intensive applications. Their strength lies in ACID compliance, ensuring reliable transactions and data integrity. Examples include MySQL and PostgreSQL, often used in applications requiring complex querying and strict data consistency, like financial systems.

NoSQL Databases

In contrast, NoSQL databases provide more flexibility in handling unstructured or semi-structured data. They come in various forms, like:

- document stores (e.g., MongoDB)

- key-value stores (e.g., Redis)

- column-family stores (e.g., Cassandra)

- graph databases (e.g., Neo4j)

These databases shine in data-intensive applications that demand horizontal scalability and rapid data processing, such as social networks and real-time analytics.

In-Memory Databases

Further considerations involve evaluating in-memory databases versus traditional disk-based storage. In-memory databases like Redis store data in RAM, offering lightning-fast access times suitable for caching and session management. However, they require careful management due to being susceptible to data loss upon power failure. Traditional disk-based storage, while slower, provides durability and is ideal for long-term data persistence.

Trade-offs between these technologies must be carefully assessed. Factors that need to be taken into account include (Dom, 2022):

- consistency

- availability

- partition tolerance,

- specific use-case requirements

Data Lifecycle Management

Another critical aspect of data engineering is managing data throughout its lifecycle, from creation to deletion. Effective data lifecycle management encompasses strategies for:

- data governance

- compliance

- archiving

- retention

- security

Data governance ensures that data management aligns with organizational policies and regulatory requirements. This includes establishing protocols for data access, quality management, and accountability. Compliance is especially important when handling sensitive data, such as personal health information or financial records, necessitating adherence to laws like the General Data Protection Regulation(GDPR) or the Health Insurance Portability and Accountability Act (HIPAA).

Data archiving and retention strategies help manage growing data volumes by moving inactive data to cost-effective storage solutions while retaining accessibility for future needs. Well-archived data is safeguarded against loss and supports compliance by preserving historical records.

Security plays a fundamental role in data lifecycle management. Implementing robust data protection measures guards against unauthorized access and breaches. Techniques include encryption, both in transit and at rest. Access control mechanisms such as passwords are used as another control measure to limit data access to authorized personnel only (*Data Engineering 101: Lifecycle, Best Practices, and Emerging Trends*, 2018).

Data Quality and Consistency

Ensuring data quality and consistency is vital for effective analysis and decision-making. High-quality data is accurate, complete, and reliable, directly impacting the insights derived from it.

Validating Data

Inconsistencies in data can lead to flawed analyses and poor decision-making. Therefore, frameworks for continuous data quality monitoring and improvement are essential. Automated tools can identify:

- anomalies

- duplicate entries

- discrepancies

This can result in timely corrections that help to maintain data integrity.

Establishing data quality metrics helps measure and improve data standards. Metrics might include error rates, data completeness ratios, and timeliness of updates, guiding ongoing enhancements in data management practices.

One technique for maintaining data quality is validation processes, which check data for accuracy and completeness during entry and processing. For instance, input validation ensures that users enter valid data formats, while process validation checks for logical consistency within data sets.

Best Practices for Data System Design

Designing data-intensive systems well is critical for managing large volumes of information efficiently. In the next section, we will look at various methods you can adopt to ensure a well-developed database. These applications demand robust design principles to ensure:

- optimal performance

- scalability

- reliability

Scalability Considerations

Scalability refers to a system's ability to handle increased loads without compromising performance. To achieve this, you must understand the difference between horizontal and vertical scaling. To recap these concepts:

- **Horizontal scaling** involves adding more machines to a pool of resources, such as adding more servers to a database cluster.

- **Vertical scaling** involves adding more power to existing machines, like upgrading a server's CPU or RAM.

Horizontal scaling is often preferred in data-intensive applications because it offers better fault tolerance and load distribution. However, it comes with its challenges, such as managing distributed data and ensuring consistency across multiple nodes.

Solutions like sharding—where data is partitioned across various databases—and implementing distributed file systems can help overcome these challenges.

Performance Testing

Performance testing is another critical area to consider when addressing scalability concerns. Regularly conducting performance tests helps identify bottlenecks that could hinder scalability. Load testing tools like Apache JMeter or Locust can simulate high user traffic, enabling developers to pinpoint weak spots and optimize them accordingly.

Modularity and Decoupling

Next, modularity and decoupling in system design should be considered. Creating modular systems makes the application easier to manage and update. This involves breaking the system into smaller, independent modules to simplify development and maintenance tasks.

Microservices

Microservices architecture exemplifies this approach. In a microservices-based system, each service runs as a separate process and communicates via well-defined APIs. This architecture improves flexibility and allows teams to deploy updates independently without affecting the entire system.

Microservicing of modules also follows the separation of concerns principle, where each module handles a specific functionality. For example, one microservice might handle user authentication while another manages data storage. This separation ensures that changes in one module do not impact others, enhancing overall system stability.

Clear interfaces between system components are crucial for effective modularization. Interfaces should be well-documented and standardized to ensure that different modules can communicate seamlessly. Using RESTful APIs or gRPC can help establish these clear communication protocols.

Performance Optimization Techniques

Optimizing performance is vital for enhancing data processing speeds and responsiveness. One effective strategy is caching.

Caching

Caching mechanisms store frequently accessed data in memory, reducing the need to fetch it from the primary database repeatedly. This significantly reduces latency and improves response times. Implementing caching at multiple layers, such as using in-memory caches like Redis or Memcached, can provide substantial performance gains.

Query optimization and indexing are also critical in database design.

- **Proper indexing** helps speed up data retrieval by allowing the database to locate the necessary records more quickly.

- **Optimizing SQL queries** to reduce complexity can minimize the load on the database, improving overall system performance.

Profiling and performance tuning are indispensable techniques for identifying and addressing inefficiencies. Profiling tools like Py-Spy or cProfile can:

- analyze code execution

- highlight time-consuming operations

Once identified, these bottlenecks can be optimized through code adjustments or resource reallocation, ensuring smoother operation and faster response times.

Monitoring and Maintenance

Effective monitoring is essential for maintaining the health of data-intensive systems. Monitoring involves tracking various metrics, such as CPU usage, memory consumption, and network traffic, to detect anomalies early. Tools like Prometheus and Grafana can provide real-time insights and visualizations, aiding in proactive system management.

Logging and alerting are integral parts of monitoring.

- **Comprehensive logging** that captures detailed events within the system, helping diagnose issues when they arise.

- **Alerting mechanisms** that notify administrators of potential problems, enabling timely intervention before they escalate.

Data observability goes beyond traditional monitoring by offering a holistic view of the system's state. It encompasses metrics, logs, and traces to provide context into how different components interact. The result helps to effectively identify the root cause of issues. This leads to a quick resolution of any issues thus identified.

Ongoing system maintenance is equally important to prevent downtime by completing regular:

- software updates

- security patches

- hardware checks

This will ensure that the system remains robust and secure.

Automating maintenance tasks can further enhance efficiency and reduce the likelihood of human error. Automation tools like Ansible and Puppet can streamline routine maintenance processes, freeing up valuable time for development and innovation.

Final Insights

Throughout the chapter, we have:

- explored the key distinctions between data-intensive and CPU-intensive systems, emphasizing their unique characteristics and suitable use cases.

- gained an understanding of the foundational concepts that are essential for making informed decisions in system design.

Knowing whether to prioritize the management or computation of data allows developers to tailor their approach based on the specific needs of their applications. This knowledge is crucial for avoiding common pitfalls that arise from mismatched system designs.

Real-world examples from industry giants like Google, Facebook, and high-frequency trading firms illuminated the practical implications of these design choices.

By leveraging best practices such as distributed databases for data-intensive tasks and parallel processing techniques for computational demands, one can optimize performance and achieve desired outcomes.

We explored how data-intensive applications focus on managing vast volumes of data through scalable and reliable methods.

A comparison was made between these and CPU-intensive systems that are geared more toward handling heavy computational tasks, often found in scientific computing and financial modeling.

Techniques such as vertical and horizontal scaling, redundancy, and fault tolerance were highlighted for building robust systems.

This chapter lays the groundwork for more advanced discussions on data engineering and system design, equipping readers with the insights needed to tackle complex challenges in their projects. The next chapter helps you prepare the groundwork for putting your knowledge into practice by teaching you how to set up your Python environment.

CHAPTER 2

Setting Up Your Python Environment for Data Analysis

Setting up your Python environment for data analysis is essential if you want to develop data-intensive applications using Python as your programming language. In this chapter, we will explore the various steps required to establish a robust development environment tailored specifically for distributed data applications. The initial setup of your programming environment can significantly influence the ease with which you manage libraries, dependencies, and versions of Python.

Installation Options: Anaconda vs. Python.org Downloads

There are two options available for installing Python. You can install the necessary packages from either Python.org or from the Anaconda site (www.anaconda.com). Each option offers distinct advantages depending on your needs. You could require greater control over package installations or opt for a convenient pre-packaged suite of essential data science libraries. We will discuss the importance of virtual environments in managing project-based dependencies, along with step-by-step guidance on creating and activating these environments using both venv and conda. Toward the end of this chapter, you will learn how to resolve common installation errors and ensure that all necessary tools are correctly configured. This will help in setting a strong foundation for your data projects.

	Python	**Anaconda**
Website	Python.org	Anaconda.com
Package Manager	PyPI	conda
Virtual Environment	venv	conda
Integrated Development Environment (IDE)	Jupyter Notebooks PyCharm Visual Studio Code Atom Spyder PyDev	 Spyder Visual Studio Code JupyterLab PyCharm

Installation of Python and Essential Libraries for Data Projects

Downloading From Python.org

Downloading Python directly from Python.org gives you the most control over your Python environment. It allows you to install the latest version and any additional packages as needed.

One critical step during this installation is to ensure that you add Python to your system PATH.

This setup lets you run Python commands directly from your terminal or command prompt.

Using Anaconda

Anaconda is a popular alternative, especially if you plan to work with data science libraries. Anaconda comes pre-packaged with many essential libraries such as Pandas, NumPy, Matplotlib, and Scikit-Learn, making it a convenient choice for data-related projects. Additionally, Anaconda includes conda, a powerful package manager that simplifies the process of installing and managing libraries.

To install Anaconda, download it from Anaconda's official website (www.anaconda.com/products/distribution). You can select the version that will work on your operating system. Once installed, you can use the conda command to create environments and manage packages efficiently.

Introduction to Essential Data Libraries

For any data project, certain libraries are indispensable. These include:

- **Pandas**: Used for data manipulation and analysis.

- **NumPy**: Fundamental package for numerical computations.

- **Matplotlib**: Essential for data visualization.

- **Scikit-Learn**: Key library for machine learning applications.

Installing Libraries Using pip

Once Python is installed, you can use pip, Python's package installer to install data libraries:

```
pip install pandas numpy matplotlib scikit-learn
```

This command will install the latest versions of these packages from the Python Package Index (PyPI).

Installing Libraries Using conda

If you opted for Anaconda, you can use conda to install these libraries. Open your terminal and type:

```
conda install pandas numpy matplotlib scikit-learn
```

Using conda ensures compatibility between packages, which can prevent potential conflicts.

Importance of Virtual Environments

Using virtual environments is vital for managing project-based dependencies. Virtual environments isolate your project's packages, preventing conflicts between different projects' requirements. There are two main tools for creating virtual environments: venv and conda.

Using venv

venv is included with Python 3.5 and later. Here's how to create and activate a virtual environment:

1. **Create a virtual environment**:

   ```bash
   python -m venv myenv
   ```

   Replace myenv with your desired environment name.

1. **Activate the virtual environment**:

- On Windows:

   ```bash
   myenv\Scripts\activate
   ```

- On macOS and Linux:

   ```bash
   source myenv/bin/activate
   ```

1. **Install necessary packages**:

   While in the activated environment:

   ```bash
   pip install pandas numpy matplotlib scikit-learn
   ```

1. **Deactivate the virtual environment**:

   Simply type:

   ```bash
   deactivate
   ```

Using conda

Creating and managing virtual environments is even more manageable with conda. Here's how:

1. **Create a virtual environment**:

   ```bash
   conda create --name myenv python=3.8
   ```

   This command creates a new environment named myenv with Python 3.8.

1. **Activate the virtual environment**:

   ```bash
   conda activate myenv
   ```

1. **Install necessary packages**:

   ```bash
   conda install pandas numpy matplotlib scikit-learn
   ```

1. **Deactivate the virtual environment**:

   ```bash
   ```

```
conda deactivate
```

Fixing Common Installation Errors

While setting up your Python environment, you might encounter some common issues. Here are some tips for troubleshooting:

Missing PATH Variable

If you get an error saying Python is not recognized, it's likely because the PATH variable was not set correctly during installation. To fix this:

- On Windows, go to System Properties > Advanced > Environment Variables and add Python's path to the PATH variable.

- On macOS/Linux, edit your .bashrc or .zshrc file to include the Python path.

Package Version Conflicts

Sometimes, you may encounter conflicts between package versions, especially if they have strict dependencies. Using virtual environments can help mitigate these issues by isolating dependencies for each project.

Installation Errors with Specific Packages

For example, if you face issues while installing scikit-learn, make sure all dependencies like numpy and scipy are installed first. For complex installations, refer to the official documentation:

- Scikit-Learn: scikit-learn.org/stable/install.html (*Installing Scikit-Learn*, n.d.)

Getting Help

If you're still facing difficulties, community support forums can be invaluable resources. Websites like Stack Overflow, Reddit's r/learnpython subreddit, and GitHub discussions offer assistance from fellow programmers and experts. Additionally, make use of the extensive documentation available for Python and its libraries, which often provide solutions to common problems.

Introduction to Integrated Development Environments (IDEs) and Jupyter Notebooks for Enhanced Coding and Data Exploration

When setting up a Python environment for data analysis, selecting the right Integrated Development Environment (IDE) is crucial. IDEs streamline coding workflows, provide debugging tools, and often include features tailored to specific programming needs.

Comparison of Popular IDEs

Starting with **PyCharm**, this IDE was developed by JetBrains and has two editions: Community (free) and Professional (paid).

PyCharm is renowned for its code completion, navigation features, and robust debugging capabilities. It supports various frameworks such as Django, Flask, and others, making it ideal for web development alongside data science projects. The integrated unit tester and support for version control systems like Git make it an excellent choice for experienced developers working in collaborative environments. Moreover, PyCharm's rich community support ensures that users can find ample tutorials and plugins to enhance their coding experience (Unite.AI, n.d.).

Visual Studio Code, another popular IDE, is developed by Microsoft and offers a highly customizable interface. Its strengths lie in its lightweight nature and extensive plugin ecosystem.

With extensions for Python, **Jupyter Notebooks**, and numerous other languages and tools, Visual Studio Code is versatile enough to accommodate the diverse needs of data scientists and software developers alike.

The live collaboration feature, which allows multiple developers to work on the same codebase in real-time, and its integration with GitHub, make Visual Studio Code a powerful tool for both individual and team projects.

Spyder, part of the Anaconda distribution, is specifically designed for data science and scientific computing. As an open-source IDE, Spyder is entirely free and provides features like

- variable explorers

- inline code execution

- advanced visualization tools

Its user-friendly interface is particularly beneficial for beginners or those focusing exclusively on data science and machine learning tasks with its seamless integration with packages like:

- NumPy

- Pandas

- Matplotlib

This makes Spyder a strong candidate for data manipulation and visualization tasks (GeeksforGeeks, 2020).

Working on Projects

When working on Python programming projects, it is best to:

- Start by clearly defining the project requirements and objectives.

- Break down the project into smaller, manageable tasks.

- Create a timeline for completion.

- Utilize a version control system like Git to track changes and collaborate effectively with others.

- Follow best practices in coding, such as adhering to PEP 8 style guidelines, writing meaningful comments, and utilizing functions and modules for better organization.

- Testing and debugging should be done continuously throughout the development process to ensure code quality.

Best Practices for Project Organization

Maintaining clean and efficient code is critical in any data project. Organizing projects systematically can help avoid confusion and enhance productivity. Begin by structuring your project directory with clear subfolders for data, scripts, notebooks, and outputs. Consistent naming conventions for files and folders can simplify navigation and collaboration.

Version control is another essential practice. Using Git, start by initializing a repository in your project directory:

```
git init
```

Commit changes regularly with meaningful messages to keep track of code evolution. For collaborating with others, platforms like GitHub or GitLab offer remote repositories where team members can push their changes.

Documentation is equally important. Commenting code effectively ensures that the logic behind coding decisions is transparent to anyone reviewing or maintaining the code. Utilizing tools like Sphinx to generate comprehensive project documentation from docstrings can further improve code clarity and usability.

Getting Started With Jupyter Notebooks

To install Jupyter, first, ensure that you have Python installed on your system. Using pip, the installation command is simple:

```
pip install notebook
```

Once installed, launch a Jupyter Notebook using the following command:

```
jupyter notebook
```

This command will open Jupyter in your default web browser, displaying a dashboard where you can create new notebooks or manage existing ones.

Jupyter Notebooks are particularly advantageous for data projects because they support inline visualization tools, allowing for immediate plotting and data exploration. This interactive coding environment helps in rapid prototyping and iterative analysis, making complex data tasks more manageable.

The Jupyter Notebooks IDE stands out due to its interactive nature and ability to combine code execution with rich text elements, equations, and visualizations.

After installation, you can enable various extensions from the Jupyter dashboard, tailoring the notebook environment to better suit your workflow.

Integrating Jupyter With Other Tools

Enhancing the functionality of Jupyter Notebooks can be achieved through integration with other tools. GitHub, for instance, can be integrated directly within Jupyter for version control. By installing the Git extension for Jupyter, you can commit, push, and pull changes without leaving the notebook interface. This integration streamlines the workflow, keeping your code up-to-date and reducing the context-switching between applications.

Additionally, integrating Jupyter with cloud services like Google Colab or Azure Notebooks can facilitate collaborative projects and leverage cloud computing resources. These platforms allow for sharing notebooks easily, providing access to computational power without local hardware constraints.

Extensions can also significantly extend the capabilities of Jupyter Notebooks. For example, the nbextensions package offers numerous enhancements such as code folding, table of contents, and spell-check. To install it, use:

```
pip    install    jupyter_contrib_nbextensionsjupyter    contrib
nbextension install --user
```

Command Line Basics Crucial for Managing Data Projects Efficiently

Command-line interfaces (CLIs) are incredibly valuable tools for data scientists and data engineers.

Understanding what a CLI is and its importance in data science is essential. Essentially, a CLI is a text-based interface that facilitates communication with the operating system. Users input text commands, which the CLI interprets and executes, performing various tasks such as running applications, navigating file systems, and handling data files.

A CLI allows users to interact with their computers by typing commands into a text interface, as opposed to using graphical interfaces (GUIs). Despite being less visually intuitive, CLIs offer heightened control, efficiency, and flexibility, which are critical for managing extensive data projects.

For data scientists, CLIs are indispensable because they allow for rapid execution of repetitive tasks, automation through scripting, better resource management, and seamless integration with version control systems like Git.

To begin working with the CLI, it's crucial to familiarize oneself with common terminal commands for file and directory management. Navigating directories is fundamental, as it helps organize data, scripts, and results systematically. Let's explore some basic and widely-used commands:

- pwd: Stands for 'print working directory' and displays the path of the current directory.

- ls: Lists all files and directories within the current directory.

- cd: Changes the directory. For instance, cd project-directory moves you into "project-directory".

- mkdir: Creates a new folder. Example: mkdir data-projects creates a directory named "data-projects".

- mv: Moves or renames files. Example: mv script.py scripts/ moves "script.py" to the "scripts" directory.

For hands-on practice, here's a step-by-step guide on navigating directories and managing files:

1. Open your terminal or command prompt.

2. Use pwd to check your current location.

3. Create a new directory for your project using mkdir data-analysis-project.

4. Navigate into this directory with cd data-analysis-project.

5. Inside this directory, create subdirectories for organization: mkdir scripts data results.

6. Move any pre-existing Python scripts into the "scripts" folder using mv ~/Downloads/my_script.py scripts/.

Running Python scripts from the command line is another vital skill. Depending on the installed Python interpreter(s), the method may vary slightly:

- To run a script with the default system Python, use: python my_script.py.

- If using Anaconda, execute scripts with a specific interpreter version, e.g., python3.8 my_script.py.

Moreover, incorporating command-line arguments into scripts can enhance functionality. For instance, suppose my_script.py processes data files. We can modify it to accept filenames as inputs:

```
import sys

if len(sys.argv) != 2:
    print("Usage: python my_script.py <filename>")
    sys.exit(1)

filename = sys.argv[1]
# Process the file named in `filename`
```

Run this enhanced script via the CLI: python my_script.py data/input.csv.

Managing software packages and dependencies is another domain where CLI proficiency is crucial. Two primary tools, pip and conda, cater to this need:

- **pip**: The default package installer for Python. For example, to install a package, you'd type pip install pandas. To upgrade an existing package: pip install --upgrade pandas.

- **conda**: Part of the Anaconda distribution, conda handles not just Python but also libraries from other languages (like R). It also manages environments, making it easy to maintain isolated setups for different projects. Here's how to use conda:

- To create an environment: conda create --name myenv python=3.8.

- To activate this environment: conda activate myenv.

- Installing packages within this environment: conda install numpy scipy matplotlib.

Dependency Management

Dependency management refers to the fact that some packages may require other packages as requirements to function optimally. Catering for this is pivotal in large projects since different packages and their versions can have compatibility constraints. Using virtual environments mitigates these issues by maintaining project-specific setups that prevent conflicts between global and project-level dependencies.

In addressing dependency management extensively, it's significant to understand the broader context.

As projects evolve, additional packages may be required, leading to potential conflicts. For instance, upgrading one library might break compatibility with others.

By encapsulating dependencies within a virtual environment (e.g., created with conda or venv), such conflicts are minimized, ensuring stable and reproducible development setups.

Here's a concrete example:

1. Create a dedicated environment for your project: conda create --prefix ./env python=3.8 pandas scikit-learn.

2. Activate this environment: conda activate ./env.

3. Add necessary packages as the project evolves: conda install seaborn jupyterlab.

Once your environment is set up and packages installed, you can easily integrate it with workflows involving Jupyter Notebooks, facilitating interactive coding and visualization without dependency issues.

Final Thoughts

In this chapter, we covered the essential steps to set up a Python environment tailored for distributed data applications. The steps that were outlined covered the downloading and installing of Python as well as the use of libraries such as Pandas and NumPy. The next chapter will explore distributed systems further. This will lay the foundation for understanding the infrastructure behind the systems you will be building.

CHAPTER 3

Distributed Systems and Architecture

Data-intensive systems work best when they are distributed across multiple physical interfaces. This is an important aspect of ensuring their reliability when engaged in parallel processing and task modularization.

When tasks are distributed across multiple servers, their systems achieve enhanced scalability, reliability, and performance while ensuring that components can be managed independently.

Understanding the intricacies of distributed systems and architecture is therefore crucial for building robust and scalable data-intensive applications.

For this reason, distributed systems have become the backbone of modern software engineering, enabling businesses to process large volumes of data efficiently. The benefit of such architectures becomes evident in scenarios like handling unexpected traffic spikes during an e-commerce sale or maintaining seamless user experiences in real-time applications.

In this chapter, we will explore the fundamental principles governing distributed systems design, focusing on scalability, reliability, decoupling of components, and performance optimization. We will explore how tools like Apache Kafka help manage real-time data streams efficiently, emphasizing its core components and stream processing capabilities.

Additionally, we will discuss Kubernetes for orchestrating containerized applications, highlighting its features for deployment, scaling, load balancing, state management, and fault tolerance. Through practical examples and insights, readers will gain a comprehensive understanding of how to leverage these technologies to build scalable and resilient data-intensive applications, ultimately preparing them for advanced roles in system design and data architecture.

Design Principles of Distributed Systems

In the landscape of modern software engineering, distributed systems have emerged as a fundamental approach for handling data-intensive applications. This section aims to shed light on the foundational principles behind designing these systems and how they can be applied effectively to achieve scalability, reliability, decoupling of components, and optimal latency and performance.

Scalability is a primary concern in designing distributed systems. The ability to grow seamlessly and manage increased loads without significant reengineering is paramount.

For example, an airline ticketing system may have to handle sudden spikes during holiday sales or during times when customers rush to secure reduced prices. Such a system must handle a sudden spike in user activity without crashing or slowing down.

Distributed systems are designed to scale out by adding more nodes to the network, thereby distributing the load across multiple servers. This horizontal scalability ensures that the system can expand its capacity to accommodate growing demands.

Similar solutions are implemented for cloud computing platforms like Amazon Web Services (AWS) that allow businesses to add more virtual machines to their pool, enabling them to handle increased traffic effortlessly.

Reliability is another pivotal principle in distributed systems design. Its assurance of consistent system performance and data accuracy despite environmental failures is crucial in a distributed environment.

Failures are inevitable—whether it's a server crash, network outage, or hardware failure. To mitigate these risks, redundant data storage and fault tolerance mechanisms are employed.

For instance, in a distributed database system, data replication ensures that copies of data are kept on different nodes. If one node fails, another can quickly take over, ensuring the system remains operational and data integrity is maintained.

Systems like Hadoop and Cassandra use replication strategies to enhance reliability, allowing data to be immediately accessible even if some nodes go offline (AlphaCodes, 2021).

Decoupling components within a distributed system helps in creating a manageable and scalable architecture. By separating services, each component can be managed, scaled, and updated independently.

This modularity not only simplifies development but also enhances the system's robustness.

Instead of building a monolithic application, where all functionalities are bundled together, microservices can be used. These break down the application into smaller, independent services. Each service handles a specific function and communicates with other services through well-defined interfaces like REST APIs.

This approach makes it easier to pinpoint and resolve issues, scale individual services based on demand, and deploy updates without impacting the entire system. Netflix's architecture is a classic example of microservices, where streaming, billing, and recommendation services operate independently yet cohesively.

Latency and performance are critical factors in the effectiveness of a distributed system. The structure of the system can significantly impact its response times.

Latency refers to the delay between a user request and the system's response. High latency can degrade the user experience, particularly in real-time applications like online gaming or financial trading platforms where timing is critical to the overall outcome.

Designing a low-latency distributed system involves:

- optimizing network protocols

- minimizing communication overhead

- placing data closer to the users

Content Delivery Networks (CDNs), such as Akamai, efficiently reduce latency by caching content at various edge locations worldwide, ensuring that users receive data from the nearest server.

Performance optimizations in distributed systems often rely on:

- efficient resource management

- load balancing and caching mechanisms

Load balancing distributes incoming requests evenly across multiple servers to prevent any single server from becoming a bottleneck. Tools like NGINX and HAProxy are commonly used to implement load balancing in web applications.

Additionally, caching mechanisms significantly improve performance by storing frequently accessed data in high-speed memory, reducing the need for repeated computations or database queries.

In-memory data stores like Redis are employed for caching, providing rapid access to data and enhancing overall system performance.

Throughput: The amount of work the system can process in a given time period is another essential aspect of performance in distributed systems. High throughput is achieved by parallelizing tasks and efficiently utilizing available resources.

Distributed computing frameworks such as Apache Spark enable parallel processing of large datasets across clusters, dramatically increasing computational speed and efficiency. By dividing tasks into smaller units and executing them concurrently, these frameworks facilitate faster data processing and analysis.

A practical understanding of these foundational principles can significantly benefit data engineers and software developers aiming to build robust and scalable data-intensive applications. For instance, when working on a real-time analytics platform, engineers might leverage the scalability of cloud infrastructure. This ensures reliability through data replication, decoupled components using microservices, and optimized latency through strategically placed data caches. Such an approach not only enhances the system's performance but also ensures it remains resilient and adaptable to future growth and changes.

Using Apache Kafka for Data Streams

Apache Kafka is a critical tool in modern distributed systems, providing an effective way to manage real-time data streams. At the heart of Kafka lies its ability to handle large volumes of data with minimal latency, making it ideal for applications that require fast and reliable data processing.

Kafka's architecture is centered around three key components:

- producers

- brokers

- consumers

Producers generate and send data messages to Kafka topics, which are logical collections inside Kafka.

Each topic can hold various partitions, allowing Kafka to handle high throughput by distributing the load across multiple servers.

Brokers are the Kafka servers that store and serve these messages to consumers upon request.

Consumers then read and process the data from these topics, ensuring that each message is handled appropriately.

One of Kafka's main strengths is its ability to produce and consume data efficiently.

To get started, you must first install Kafka on your system.

Begin by downloading and extracting the latest Kafka version. To start the Kafka environment, generate a cluster ID and format the log directories before launching the Kafka server. This setup creates a basic Kafka environment that is ready for use.

For further instructions on installing Kafka, you can refer to the instructions near the back of the book in the *Installation Steps* section.

Topics

The next step involves creating a topic where your data events will be stored. By crafting specific commands, you can define topics tailored to your application needs. Once a topic is created, you can begin writing events into it using Kafka's console producer client. This client facilitates the input of various events, which Kafka will immediately store in the designated topic.

Consumers play a crucial role in retrieving and processing these data events. Using the console consumer client, applications can read messages from Kafka topics and process them accordingly. The real-time nature of this process ensures that data is processed as soon as it is available, making Kafka an ideal choice for time-sensitive applications.

Data Streams

Stream processing with Kafka Streams brings another layer of sophistication to data handling. Kafka Streams is a Java library designed specifically for building stream-processing applications.

Kafka Streams simplifies complex tasks by offering built-in functions to filter, aggregate, transform, and enrich data streams. For example, one can perform operations such as joining streams, windowing data into specific time frames, and maintaining stateful transformations seamlessly within Kafka Streams. This level of functionality enables developers to build robust applications that can handle vast quantities of data while maintaining low latency and high throughput.

Unlike traditional batch processing, Kafka Streams allows for continuous computation over data streams, enabling applications to react to incoming data instantly. This stream processing capability is vital for scenarios like real-time analytics, monitoring, or any application needing immediate processing of data.

Monitoring and Managing

Monitoring and managing Kafka instances is essential to ensure a healthy and efficient Kafka environment. Regularly checking the status of Kafka brokers, topics, and partitions helps prevent potential issues before they escalate.

Tools like Kafka Manager, Confluent Control Center, and Embedded JMX metrics provide comprehensive insights into the Kafka ecosystem.

They enable administrators to:

- monitor performance metrics

- track message throughput

- oversee topic partitioning

Efficient Apache Kafka management also involves strategies for scaling and fault tolerance. By adding more brokers to your Kafka cluster, you can balance the load and enhance the system's capacity to handle higher volumes of data. Additionally, configuring replication factors for topics ensures that data remains accessible even if some brokers fail.

Kubernetes (K8s) for Managing Containerized Applications

The rise of data-intensive applications has brought significant challenges in managing and orchestrating containerized environments. Kubernetes, also known as K8s, has emerged as a powerful tool for handling these tasks. This subpoint delves into how Kubernetes can be used effectively to manage containerized applications in data-intensive environments.

Introduction to Kubernetes

The Kubernetes platform builds upon years of experience from Google's production workloads combined with best-of-breed ideas from the community.

It is an open-source platform designed to automate the:

- deployment

- scaling

- operation of application containers

It groups containers that make up an application into logical units for easy management and discovery. Understanding its core concepts and architecture is crucial for anyone aiming to leverage its full potential. Central to Kubernetes are the concepts of:

- pods

- nodes

- clusters

A pod represents a group of one or more containers, sharing storage and network resources, which ensures they operate efficiently together.

Nodes are the worker machines that run the containers, while **the cluster** is the aggregation of all nodes managed by Kubernetes.

Deploying Applications on Kubernetes

Deploying applications on Kubernetes involves several steps, but let's focus on deploying a Python application to provide practical guidance.

First, you need to create a Docker image of your application.

(If you do not know how to create a Docker Image, you can refer to the *Installation Steps* section at the back of this book).

Write a Dockerfile specifying the environment setup, dependencies, and commands to run the application.

Once the Docker image is built, push it to a container registry such as Docker Hub.

Next, create Kubernetes manifests which define the deployment configuration. In order to do this, you will need to have Kubernetes installed on your system.

(If you do not know how to install Kubernetes, you can refer to the *Installation Steps* section at the back of this book).

The manifest files typically include Deployment, Service, and ConfigMap YAML files. The Deployment file specifies:

- the application's replicas

- the Docker image to use

- rolling update strategies

The Service file sets up networking rules to expose the application internally or externally.

Finally, apply these manifests using the kubectl apply -f command and Kubernetes will handle the rest—from launching the containers to ensuring their availability.

Scaling and Load Balancing

One of Kubernetes' strongest features is its capability to scale applications dynamically to meet varying loads. Horizontal Pod Autoscaling (HPA) allows Kubernetes to automatically adjust the number of running pods based on observed CPU utilization or other custom metrics.

For instance, if your Python application experiences a spike in traffic, HPA can increase the number of pods to distribute the load more evenly. This auto-scaling ensures high availability and optimal resource usage without manual intervention.

Additionally, Kubernetes includes built-in load balancing to distribute network traffic. Each service gets its own IP address and DNS name, simplifying service discovery.

As requests come in, Kubernetes intelligently routes them across multiple pods, ensuring consistent performance and reliability even as demands fluctuate.

Managing Application State and Data

While Kubernetes excels at handling stateless applications, managing stateful applications presents unique challenges.

Stateful applications require persistent storage to maintain data integrity across restarts and failures.

Kubernetes addresses the challenge of stateful applications through features like:

Persistent volumes (PVs) abstract storage provisioning, allowing different types of storage systems to integrate seamlessly. They ensure data persists beyond the lifecycle of individual pods.

StatefulSets provides each pod with a stable network identity and persistent storage, which is critical for applications like databases that depend on a consistent state.

Tools like MySQL or PostgreSQL can be deployed using StatefulSets, ensuring that each instance retains its state despite scaling operations.

Dynamic Storage

Moreover, Kubernetes supports dynamic storage provisioning, meaning storage resources can be allocated on the fly to meet growing demands. This flexibility makes Kubernetes an ideal choice for managing data-intensive workloads.

Kubernetes also provides robust mechanisms for self-healing and fault tolerance. When a pod fails, Kubernetes automatically replaces it, ensuring minimal disruption to the application. Health checks determine the readiness and liveliness of pods, and only those that pass are considered available for serving traffic. This capability is particularly vital for stateful applications where data consistency and availability are paramount.

Sensitive Information

Secret and configuration management is another important aspect where Kubernetes shines. Managing sensitive information such as database passwords or API keys can be challenging.

With Kubernetes Secrets, you can store and manage sensitive information such as passwords and tokens securely. This avoids hardcoding secrets in your application code or container images.

Furthermore, ConfigMaps allows you to decouple configuration artifacts from the application itself, facilitating easier updates and modifications without rebuilding the image.

Concluding Thoughts

This chapter has explored the design principles essential for building modern distributed systems, emphasizing scalability, reliability, decoupling of components, and performance optimization. By understanding these principles, data engineers, software developers, and job seekers can better design and manage robust, scalable applications.

Further, this chapter discussed the practical applications of Apache Kafka and Kubernetes for managing data streams and containerized environments.

Apache Kafka offers a robust solution for real-time data processing with minimal latency, making it ideal for dynamic applications.

On the other hand, Kubernetes provides powerful orchestration capabilities for deploying, scaling, and managing containerized applications.

Together, these tools help streamline the development and deployment processes, ensuring high availability, optimal resource usage, and efficient performance management. By leveraging these advanced technologies, readers are well-equipped to tackle the complexities of modern distributed systems.

As you continue exploring in the next chapter, you will learn how these systems facilitate the access and manipulation of data to provide meaningful solutions that impact daily activities.

CHAPTER 4

Data Manipulation and Analysis

Manipulating and analyzing data in Python involves using powerful libraries that streamline the handling of complex datasets.

Mastering these libraries enables you to perform sophisticated data operations that transform raw information into valuable insights.

Whether you're dealing with massive amounts of structured or unstructured data, effective manipulation techniques are crucial for extracting meaningful patterns and trends.

In this chapter, you will discover:

- The core aspects of data manipulation and analysis using Python's robust toolkit.

- How to leverage the Pandas library to create and manage DataFrames, providing a flexible structure for your data.

- Accessing and modifying specific subsets

- Data cleaning methods to ensure your results are accurate and reliable.

- Performing aggregations and group-by operations.

You'll gain practical skills that are essential for high-level data work. By the end, you'll be well-equipped to handle and analyze large-scale datasets in your projects.

Introduction to Pandas DataFrames

A DataFrame in Pandas is a tabular structure, similar to a spreadsheet or SQL table, but far more potent in terms of functionality.

This construct is central to efficient data manipulation and analysis, as it supports complex operations involving:

- data cleaning

- transformation

- aggregation

Understanding DataFrames is essential because it allows users to manage and interpret large datasets seamlessly.

Within the realm of Python, Pandas DataFrames offers a robust framework for data manipulation and analysis, an essential skill for any aspiring data engineer or systems designer.

Before diving into the myriad ways to leverage DataFrames, it is imperative to comprehend what they are and how they function.

With libraries like Pandas in Python, DataFrames are:

- two-dimensional

- size-mutable

- potentially heterogeneous

- tabular data structures

- with labeled axes (rows and columns)

- commonly used in data analysis

They function by allowing users to store and manipulate structured data across different datasets in a flexible way, enabling operations such as:

- indexing

- filtering

- aggregating

- joining data

One of the foundational skills involving DataFrames is creating them from various sources. Create a DataFrame using lists, which might be useful for small-scale, manually-input datasets. Here's a simple example:

```
import pandas as pd

data = [['Alice', 24], ['Bob', 27], ['Charlie', 22]]
df = pd.DataFrame(data, columns=['Name', 'Age'])
print(df)
```

The above code snippet generates a basic DataFrame with names and ages as columns. This simple operation illustrates the flexibility of DataFrames in handling structured data.

Dictionaries

Another common method to create DataFrames is from dictionaries. Dictionaries provide a natural and readable way to handle labeled data:

```
data = {'Name': ['Dave', 'Eva', 'Frank'], 'Age': [28, 31,
25]}
```

```
df = pd.DataFrame(data)
print(df)
```

This approach can handle larger datasets more effectively, aligning column labels with corresponding data series directly.

DataFrames can also be created from external files such as CSVs, Excel files, and even databases.

Importing data from these sources is crucial for handling real-world datasets, typically much larger and more complex than those we can manually input.

Use the command below to read data from a CSV file. It facilitates the initial steps in any data analysis pipeline, making the process instantaneous.

```
df = pd.read_csv('data.csv')
print(df.head())
```

Once a DataFrame is created, accessing and modifying the data within it is another critical skill. Indexing and filtering allow users to zero in on specific subsets of their data. For example, to access a single column, you could write:

```
ages = df['Age']
print(ages)
```

To filter rows based on a condition, you can use Boolean indexing:

```
adults = df[df['Age'] > 18]
print(adults)
```

These techniques can empower you to extract meaningful insights and focus on relevant data without altering the original dataset.

Maintaining Clean Data

Another noteworthy feature of Pandas DataFrames is their ability to maintain clean, structured data, which is paramount for optimal analysis.

Ensuring data integrity involves addressing:

- missing values

- redundant information

- inconsistent formats

One common practice is to handle missing data by either filling or dropping it:

```
df = df.fillna(method='ffill')
# Or alternatively
df = df.dropna()
```

Cleaning data not only improves the quality of the analysis but also prepares the dataset for more sophisticated transformations and modeling.

Renaming columns helps retain clarity and consistency while maintaining a structured format:

```
df.rename(columns={'Age': 'Years'}, inplace=True)
print(df)
```

This step, though seemingly minor, can significantly enhance the dataset's readability and usability, especially when dealing with extensive data operations.

Performing Aggregations and GroupBy Operations

Data Aggregation

Aggregating data is a cornerstone in the field of data analysis. It involves combining multiple pieces of information into a single summary or result, which helps reveal trends and patterns within datasets.

Aggregation functions, including sum, average, count, min, and max, are tools for performing various data operations.

For example, if you have a dataset that captures daily sales figures over a year, an aggregation function can help you determine monthly sales totals or average daily sales per month. This ability to condense large amounts of data into meaningful summaries is invaluable for understanding overall performance and making informed decisions.

Understanding the significance of aggregation functions requires examining their practical applications. These functions allow analysts to discern high-level trends and outliers within the data. For instance, calculating the average temperature over several years can highlight climate change patterns while summing up quarterly revenue reveals a company's financial performance over time.

The power of aggregation lies in its ability to simplify complex datasets into actionable insights, thereby supporting strategic planning and operational efficiency.

The GroupBy Function

Moving on to the GroupBy function, which plays a crucial role in data segmentation. GroupBy is a powerful operation available in the Pandas library that enables users to split data into distinct groups based on specific criteria before performing aggregation.

Imagine a situation with a dataset consisting of sales transactions. These might include:

- product categories

- prices

- dates

Using the GroupBy function, you can segment this data by product category and then apply aggregation functions to calculate total sales per category. This segmentation facilitates targeted analysis, helping identify which product lines are performing well and which ones need attention.

To illustrate how GroupBy works, consider a dataset containing employee details, including departments and salaries. Computing the average salary for each department can be calculated by grouping the data by department and then applying an aggregation function like the mean. This focused analysis allows for a deeper understanding of departmental salary structures, highlighting disparities that may require intervention.

Combining aggregation functions with GroupBy operations unleashes the full potential of data analysis. This combination provides a more granular view of the data, uncovering insights that might be missed when looking at the dataset as a whole.

When analyzing a company's total sales, you can use the GroupBy function to segment by region and aggregate the results. This can reveal which regions are driving growth and which are lagging behind, providing an understanding of the available data that goes beyond the company's total sales. This level of detail is essential for data-driven decision-making, allowing organizations to tailor their strategies to different segments of their market effectively.

When applying aggregation functions to grouped data, it's beneficial to follow some key techniques to maximize insights.

- First, always ensure your data is clean and properly formatted; any inconsistencies can skew your results.

- Next, choose the right aggregation functions that align with your analysis goals. Sum and mean are commonly used, but depending on your needs, other functions like median, variance, or custom aggregates might be more appropriate.

- Additionally, leveraging multiple aggregation functions simultaneously can provide a comprehensive view of the data.

For example, computing both the count and mean of sales transactions per region can indicate not only where the most transactions occur but also the average transaction value, offering a dual perspective on performance.

Practical Examples

Do this exercise to solidify the concepts of aggregation and GroupBy techniques.

- Create a simple scenario whereby your dataset contains customer purchase records, including customer IDs, purchase amounts, and dates.

- Populate your database with random data that you can work with to test the concepts you are learning.

- Once you have set this up, group the data by customer ID and apply the sum aggregation function to calculate the total spend per customer.

This exercise will help you understand how much each customer contributes to overall revenue, thus aiding customer value assessment. To add complexity, group by both customer ID and month to analyze monthly spending patterns per customer, illustrating seasonal or behavioral trends.

Another exercise to test your skills involves working with a dataset capturing website traffic data, including visitor IDs, page views, and visit durations.

- Set up the dataset to accommodate website data that records visitor IDs, page views, and visit duration. This is the type of data that you would typically encounter if you were managing a website.

- Populate the dataset with appropriate random data.

- Thereafter, group the data by visitor ID and apply aggregation functions like count (to tally page views) and mean (to calculate average visit duration) to derive insights into user engagement levels.

This analysis informs strategies to enhance user experience and retention.

Practicing these techniques can help you understand the practical utility of aggregation and GroupBy operations. To reinforce the versatility of these methods, try working with diverse datasets such as sales, customer behavior, or operational metrics. This will help you enhance your problem-solving skills and deepen your comprehension of core data analysis principles.

Visualizing Data With Matplotlib and Seaborn

Data visualization plays a pivotal role in interpreting and making sense of complex datasets. It transforms data into a visual context, such as graphs or charts, making the data easier to understand and more accessible. Effective visuals can communicate trends, patterns, and outliers much more clearly than raw data, thereby enhancing analytical effectiveness. Understanding these insights quickly and accurately is essential for data-driven decision-making.

You can use Matplotlib to plot your data. Matplotlib is one of the most widely used libraries in Python for generating simple visualizations such as line, bar, and scatter plots. This is foundational to your exploration of data visualization concepts. These plots form the basis for understanding data distributions and relationships between variables. For example:

- Line plots are ideal for displaying trends over time.

- Bar plots are useful when comparing quantities across different categories.

- Scatter plots are excellent for identifying correlations between two variables.

Here's a simple example of how to create a basic line plot with Matplotlib:

```
import matplotlib.pyplot as plt

x = [1, 2, 3, 4, 5]
y = [2, 3, 5, 7, 11]

plt.plot(x, y)
plt.xlabel('X-axis Label')
plt.ylabel('Y-axis Label')
plt.title('Simple Line Plot')
plt.show()
```

By mastering these basic plots, you can gain confidence in creating initial visualizations that will help you start to understand your data better.

Heatmaps

Heatmaps in Python are graphical representations of data where individual values are represented as colors. They allow for the visualization of complex data matrixes and patterns within the dataset.

When creating Heatmaps, you can use Seaborn. This is an alternative to Matplotlib that offers more sophisticated and aesthetically pleasing visualizations.

Seaborn simplifies the process of creating complex statistical graphics, making it easier to generate attractive and informative visuals. One notable feature of Seaborn is its ability to create Heatmaps.

Heatmaps are great for showing the correlation between variables and highlighting interactions within a dataset. To illustrate, consider a scenario where you have a dataset containing columns for "Overall," "Age," "wage_euro," and "Skill Moves." You can calculate the correlation between these variables and visualize it using a heatmap as per the below example:

```
import seaborn as sns
import pandas as pd

# Sample DataFrame
data = {'Overall': [85, 88, 76, 90, 80],
        'Age': [22, 23, 21, 25, 24],
        'wage_euro': [200000, 250000, 150000, 300000,
100000],
        'Skill Moves': [4, 5, 3, 5, 4]}
df = pd.DataFrame(data)

corr = df.corr()
sns.heatmap(corr, annot=True)
plt.title('Heatmap of Overall, Age, wage_euro, and Skill
Moves')
plt.show()
```

(Pierre, 2023)

The resultant Heatmap clearly visualizes how each pair of variables relates to one another, which can be indispensable for identifying key insights at a glance.

Seaborn also includes categorical plots such as:

- bar plots

- box plots

- violin plots

These plots are particularly useful for summarizing data according to categorical values.

For instance, a box plot can provide a clear summary of the distribution of data points by showing their medians and quartiles, which helps in identifying any potential outliers. Here's a simple example of creating a box plot (Pierre, 2023):

```
sns.boxplot(x='variable', y='value', data=pd.melt(df))
plt.title('Box Plot Example')
plt.xlabel('Variable')
plt.ylabel('Value')
plt.show()
```

Integrating Matplotlib and Seaborn allows you to leverage the strengths of both libraries. While Matplotlib offers fine-grained control over your plots, Seaborn makes it easier to produce visually appealing statistical graphics. Combining the two can result in comprehensive visual narratives that effectively communicate the story behind your data. Here's an example of how you might combine both libraries (Pierre, 2023):

```
fig, ax = plt.subplots()
sns.scatterplot(x='Age', y='Overall', data=df, ax=ax)
ax.set_title('Scatter Plot with Seaborn and Matplotlib')
ax.set_xlabel('Age')
ax.set_ylabel('Overall')
plt.show()
```

In this example, Seaborn creates the scatter plot while Matplotlib sets the title and labels, thus combining the best of both worlds.

Customizing and refining visuals is crucial for clarity and professionalism. You can customize your graphic output by adjusting plot colors, adding titles and labels, and modifying the layout to suit specific requirements. By doing so, you can ensure that the visuals not only look good but also convey the intended message accurately. For instance, let's customize the previous scatter plot by adding different colors and markers based on another variable (Pierre, 2023):

```
sns.scatterplot(x='Age', y='Overall', hue='Skill Moves',
style='Skill Moves', data=df)
plt.title('Customized Scatter Plot')
```

```
plt.xlabel('Age')
plt.ylabel('Overall')
plt.legend(title='Skill Moves')
plt.show()
```

In this plot, the color and style of the markers vary according to the 'Skill Moves' column, providing an extra layer of information. Such customizations enhance the plot's interpretability and make it more engaging for the viewer.

By integrating these techniques, you can create sophisticated visual narratives that effectively communicate your findings. Understanding how to use both Matplotlib and Seaborn will empower you to craft professional-quality visualizations. This is invaluable for presenting data findings in reports, dashboards, and presentations, where clarity and aesthetics significantly impact the effectiveness of communication.

Final Thoughts

Python's powerful libraries, especially Pandas, allow for efficient data manipulation and analysis, which are essential skills for any aspiring data professional. In this chapter, we explored how DataFrames can be created from various sources, such as lists, dictionaries, and external files like CSVs.

We also delved into accessing and modifying data within DataFrames through indexing and filtering techniques. These foundational skills enable users to manage large datasets effectively, ensuring clean and structured data ready for further analysis.

Moreover, we examined the importance of aggregation and GroupBy operations in summarizing and segmenting data. By leveraging these features, analysts can uncover meaningful insights and patterns that might otherwise go unnoticed.

Practical exercises highlighted in this chapter offered hands-on experience with real-world datasets, reinforcing the utility of these techniques. By mastering these concepts, readers are equipped to handle complex data manipulation tasks and extract valuable insights, setting a strong foundation for advanced data analysis and visualization in subsequent chapters. The next chapter adds to this knowledge by teaching you how to optimize data systems so that you maximize the use of the resources available to you.

CHAPTER 5

Optimizing Data Systems

O ptimizing data systems involves implementing a variety of strategies designed to enhance performance and reliability. These strategies are crucial to ensuring that data flows smoothly through the system, reducing delays, and preventing potential failures that could have significant impacts on business operations. By focusing on identifying and resolving bottlenecks, effective monitoring, and using advanced tools, organizations can significantly improve their data processing capabilities.

In this chapter, we will explore several key techniques for optimizing data systems. We'll begin by examining:

- how to identify bottlenecks in data processing

- understanding their causes

- the broad effects they have on system performance and costs

The chapter also discusses common issues such as slow queries, network latency, and resource contention, offering practical solutions like query optimization and investing in robust network infrastructure.

Additionally, we'll discuss the importance of continuous monitoring using tools like Prometheus and Grafana, as well as profiling applications with tools like Apache JMeter to ensure optimal performance. Throughout the chapter, real-world examples and case studies will illustrate the effectiveness of these optimization strategies, providing you with actionable insights into enhancing your own data systems.

Identifying Bottlenecks in Data Processing

Understanding Bottlenecks

A bottleneck in a data processing system refers to a point where the flow of data is significantly impeded, leading to slower processing speeds and potentially compromising the entire system's performance.

The concept is similar to a scenario where five lanes on a highway merge into one, causing traffic to slow down drastically and resulting in delays. Likewise, in data systems, bottlenecks create critical points of congestion that hinder data flow and reduce efficiency. Identifying and understanding these bottlenecks is pivotal for optimizing data systems.

To grasp the full impact of bottlenecks on data processing, it's essential to recognize their broad effects. When data processing slows, it can delay insights and decision-making, which are crucial for businesses relying on timely information. Additionally, bottlenecks can lead to increased operational costs as systems struggle to process backlogged data, requiring more resources and time.

In severe cases, these performance issues can result in data loss or corruption, further aggravating the situation. Recognizing and addressing bottlenecks isn't just about improving speed; it's also about maintaining the integrity and reliability of data systems.

Common Causes of Bottlenecks

Several factors can contribute to bottlenecks in data systems.

Slow queries are a common culprit. When a database query takes too long to execute, it holds up the entire data processing chain.

Optimizing these queries through indexing, query restructuring, and proper resource allocation can alleviate some of these issues. These solutions are beneficial for different reasons. Indexing a database that is constantly being used for information retrieval makes it easier to find data.

When indexes are used, each entry has a unique index, making it easier to identify and operate on. Query restructuring ensures that your queries are not made redundant by over-specifying requirements.

The simpler the query is, the faster it will be to execute it. You can further improve processing speed by assigning priority to different tasks and giving them preference over those tasks that do not require immediate responses.

You can also further distribute the processing of queries across resources. This will assist in

Network latency is another typical cause. If the network cannot handle the volume of data traffic efficiently, delays ensue.

Investing in robust network infrastructure that supports high-speed data transfer can mitigate latency issues. Moreover, distributed computing methods can help by spreading the workload across multiple nodes, minimizing the risk of bottlenecks.

Resource contention happens when multiple processes compete for the same resources, such as:

- CPU

- memory

- disk I/O

Properly configuring and scaling your hardware resources to match the demand can resolve these contentions.

Load balancing techniques can distribute workloads evenly across servers, ensuring no single server becomes a bottleneck. To prevent resource contention, it's crucial to monitor resource usage continuously and make adjustments as needed.

Monitoring Tools and Techniques

Effective monitoring is vital for identifying and resolving bottlenecks.

Some standard approaches you can follow to preemptively identify bottlenecks include:

- implementing comprehensive logging for all critical operations in your data system

- utilize performance monitoring tools to track KPIs

- set up alerts for anomalies

- regularly profile your applications under various load conditions

Logging is a fundamental monitoring method that provides detailed records of all system activities.

By analyzing logs, you can pinpoint the exact moments and locations where bottlenecks occur. To avoid future bottlenecks, logs can:

- offer invaluable historical data

- enable trend analysis

- enable proactive measures

Performance metrics are equally important. Tools like Prometheus, Grafana, and Elasticsearch stack (ELK) provide real-time monitoring and visualization of key performance indicators (KPIs) such as:

- CPU utilization

- memory usage

- network throughput

These tools help you visualize data flow and quickly identify any abnormal patterns indicative of bottlenecks (Dremio, 2023).

Profiling tools like Apache JMeter and VisualVM offer in-depth analysis of application performance. They help you understand how different components interact and where potential bottlenecks might be lurking. For example, JMeter allows you to:

- simulate heavy loads on your application

- observe how it handles stress

- identify weak points that could turn into bottlenecks under real-world conditions.

Case Study of Bottleneck Resolution

The following case study involves an e-commerce company experiencing frequent slowdowns during peak shopping seasons. The primary issue was traced back to slow database queries. Initially, the team used basic logging to monitor application performance, but the logs were too voluminous to analyze effectively. They decided to implement more advanced monitoring tools, including Prometheus and Grafana, to visualize performance metrics in real-time.

Through these tools, they identified that specific queries were taking significantly longer to execute during peak periods.

Using SQL profiling tools, they pinpointed poorly optimized queries and high lock contention on certain tables. The solution that was eventually implemented involved:

- creating appropriate indexes.

- rewriting inefficient queries.

- partitioning large tables to balance the load.

- upgrading the network infrastructure to handle increased traffic and implementing load balancers to distribute requests evenly across multiple servers.

After these optimizations, the company saw a dramatic improvement in its system's performance.

Query execution times decreased by 70%, and the overall system throughput increased by 50%. During the following peak shopping season, the system handled traffic smoothly without significant slowdowns, illustrating the effectiveness of its bottleneck resolution strategies (Urban, 2018).

This case study underscores the importance of a systematic approach to identifying and resolving bottlenecks.

Leveraging advanced monitoring tools and implementing targeted optimizations can significantly enhance the performance and reliability of data systems.

Caching and Data Storage Strategies

By employing effective caching methods and storage strategies, you can increase the delivery of solutions to your users, thus providing them with a better experience.

Caching can play a vital role in enhancing the performance and reliability of the data systems you manage. By understanding the purpose of caching, exploring different caching strategies, and examining various data storage solutions, you can design systems that are both efficient and robust.

Firstly, let's delve into the purpose of caching. Caching is a technique for storing copies of frequently accessed data in a location that allows for quick retrieval.

The primary benefit of caching is the significant improvement in data processing speed. When data is stored in a cache, it can be retrieved much faster than from the original source, reducing latency and enabling quicker response times.

For instance, think about how often-used web pages load faster on subsequent visits; this is because they are retrieved from your browser's cache rather than being downloaded anew from the server. In data systems, similar principles apply, leading to optimized performance and better user experience.

Database caching involves storing query results in the cache to reduce the load on the database when the same query is executed multiple times.

This can dramatically speed up retrieval times for frequently requested data. For example, if you have a high-traffic website that frequently runs the same complex queries to display certain information, caching those query results can save considerable processing time and database resources.

Database Caching

Database caching can utilize distributed caching to store data on various nodes on the network, while memory caching stores data in the user's system RAM.

This method offers extremely fast access times since retrieving data from memory is quicker than retrieving it from disk storage on a remote server.

An example of memory caching is using Redis, an open-source in-memory data structure store that is widely used for caching purposes.

Implementing Caching

Implementation considerations are crucial for effectively deploying caching layers. Begin by identifying which data should be cached.

Frequently accessed and read-heavy data makes for ideal data candidates. For practical steps, first, assess the data access patterns within your application. Determine which parts of the data are repeatedly accessed and which are relatively static.

For example, product catalog data on an e-commerce site changes infrequently but is read continuously, making it an excellent candidate for caching.

Once identified, implement the caching layer by choosing an appropriate caching strategy suited to your application's requirements. For instance, a combination of client-side caching (using HTTP cache headers and local storage) and server-side caching (in-memory caching with tools like Memcached or database caching) can provide a robust caching solution.

Client-side caching ensures that data doesn't need to travel over the network for every request, while server-side caching helps handle increased traffic and complex data access patterns efficiently (Thomas, 2023).

As you implement your caching strategy, keep in mind the importance of ensuring the consistency of cached data.

In distributed systems, different instances of an application may hold outdated versions of the data. Implementing a shared caching strategy can help mitigate these issues. Shared caches keep all application instances synchronized but come with added complexity and potential latency (Microsoft, n.d.).

Data Storage Solutions

Moving on to data storage solutions, different types cater to various needs.

Relational databases, like MySQL or PostgreSQL, are traditional and structured around tables and relationships between data points. These are highly reliable and suitable for applications requiring transactional integrity and complex querying capabilities.

NoSQL databases, such as MongoDB and Cassandra, offer more flexible schemas and are designed to handle large volumes of unstructured or semi-structured data.

They are often favored for their scalability and ability to manage big data scenarios effectively. For instance, social media platforms that deal with vast amounts of user-generated content often utilize NoSQL databases due to their ability to scale out horizontally.

Data lakes are another solution to consider. They serve as centralized repositories that store raw data in its native format until it is needed.

This approach is particularly advantageous for big data analytics, where you might need to process and analyze vast datasets to uncover insights. Azure Data Lake and Amazon S3 are popular choices for implementing data lakes.

Protection and Performance

Security is an important consideration for cached data as it is stored outside of the security infrastructure that protects the main servers.

To protect cached data from unauthorized access, mechanisms such as authentication and encryption must be implemented.

Applications should specify which identities can access and manipulate the cached data, thus ensuring that sensitive information remains secure even in the cache.

Finally, monitor and fine-tune your caching strategy. Use performance metrics to understand the impact of caching on your system and make adjustments as needed.

Effective monitoring can highlight areas where the cache hits, cache misses, and stale data affect performance, allowing for continuous optimization.

Load Balancing and Distributed Computing

In the realm of data systems, creating scalable solutions is essential to managing increasing workloads and ensuring reliability.

One of the key strategies for achieving this is through load balancing and distributed computing. This section explores these concepts, shedding light on their benefits and practical implementations for building robust data systems.

Understanding load balancing is a fundamental step in optimizing data systems that work across distributed systems.

At its core, load balancing refers to the process of distributing incoming network traffic across multiple servers to ensure no single server becomes overwhelmed.

The primary purpose of load balancing is to:

- enhance system performance and reliability.

- prevent bottlenecks.

- reduce the risk of server failure.

By distributing workloads more evenly, load balancing can also lead to improved response times and increased resource availability, making it a critical component for maintaining seamless operations.

Types of Load Balancers

There are various types of load balancers, each with distinct functionalities and use cases. **Hardware load balancers** are physical devices designed to manage network traffic. These devices are often used in high-traffic environments where performance and reliability are paramount. They offer robust features such as SSL offloading, which can free up resources on application servers to improve overall efficiency.

Software load balancers, on the other hand, are applications that run on standard hardware or virtual machines.

They direct the flow of traffic to make sure that it is evenly distributed between servers. This provides flexibility and scalability when traffic volumes increase, thus allowing organizations to adapt quickly to changing workloads.

Software load balancers can be deployed in cloud environments, offering elastic scaling capabilities that automatically adjust based on traffic demands. This adaptability makes them an attractive choice for modern, dynamic applications.

DNS load balancing utilizes Domain Name System (DNS) to distribute traffic across multiple servers.

When a client makes a request, the DNS system directs it to one of several IP addresses associated with the domain name.

This method offers a simple and effective way to balance loads without the need for additional hardware or software. However, it may not provide the same level of granularity and control as dedicated load balancers.

Moving beyond load balancing, Distributed Computing Concepts play a pivotal role in designing scalable data systems.

Horizontal scaling, for instance, involves adding more servers to handle increased workloads rather than upgrading existing ones. This approach allows systems to grow seamlessly and manage vast amounts of data efficiently.

Data partitioning is another crucial aspect of distributed computing. It entails dividing a large dataset into smaller, more manageable pieces, which can be processed in parallel across multiple servers.

This division enables faster data processing and improves system responsiveness. Data partitioning can be implemented using various techniques, such as sharding in databases, which distributes data across different nodes based on predefined criteria.

Load Balancing Case Studies

Google Infrastructure

To illustrate the effectiveness of load balancing and distributed computing, we can turn to Case Studies on Load Balancing in Action.

One notable example is Google's search engine infrastructure. Google employs advanced load-balancing techniques to manage billions of search queries daily.

By leveraging a combination of hardware and software load balancers, Google ensures rapid query responses and high availability. Their distributed computing architecture facilitates horizontal scaling, enabling the system to handle ever-growing data volumes efficiently.

Netflix's Content Delivery

Another real-world implementation is Netflix's content delivery network (CDN). Netflix uses load balancing to distribute streaming video content across numerous servers globally.

This distribution minimizes latency and ensures high-quality viewing experiences for users. Additionally, Netflix employs distributed computing principles to manage and deliver vast amounts of video data effectively. By partitioning content and distributing it across geographically dispersed servers, Netflix achieves redundancy and fault tolerance, ensuring uninterrupted service even during peak demand.

Amazon Web Services Elastic Load Balancing

Amazon Web Services (AWS) provides another compelling case study. AWS Elastic Load Balancing (ELB) offers a suite of load-balancing services tailored to different needs.

From simple web applications to complex, multi-tier architectures, ELB helps distribute traffic efficiently by ensuring that all servers are utilized to capacity. AWS also exemplifies distributed computing through its extensive use of microservices architecture, where applications are decomposed into smaller, independent services. This decomposition allows for horizontal scaling and easier management of individual components.

These case studies demonstrate how load balancing and distributed computing are integral to building scalable, reliable data systems. By distributing workloads and leveraging horizontal scaling and data partitioning, organizations can achieve significant improvements in performance and resilience.

In summary, understanding load balancing and adopting distributed computing concepts are essential for optimizing data systems. Load balancing ensures even distribution of traffic, preventing server overloads and enhancing system reliability.

Different types of load balancers, including hardware, software, and DNS, offer unique advantages tailored to various scenarios. Meanwhile, distributed computing principles like horizontal scaling and data partitioning enable efficient handling of large datasets and seamless system growth.

Bringing It All Together

In this chapter, we focused on identifying and addressing bottlenecks in data processing systems. Recognizing the critical points where data flow is impeded allows for targeted optimizations that enhance system performance and reliability.

We examined common causes of bottlenecks, such as slow queries, network latency, and resource contention. Practical strategies like query optimization, robust network infrastructure, and load balancing were identified as ways to significantly improve data throughput.

Combining this with monitoring using tools like logging, performance metrics, and profiling provides valuable insights to preemptively address bottlenecks in the future.

The case study illustrated how an e-commerce company improved its system's performance by identifying slow database queries and optimizing both the network infrastructure and resource distribution.

These techniques not only enhanced processing speeds but helped maintain the integrity and reliability of the data systems, ensuring they could handle peak loads without compromising performance.

Understanding and implementing these strategies is crucial for data engineers and developers aiming to create efficient, reliable, data-intensive applications.

In the next chapter, we discuss data sources and how to efficiently create data pipelines for handling large volumes of data. You will learn how to effectively load this data for analysis and transformation into practical solutions.

CHAPTER 6

Building Data Pipelines With Python

Building data pipelines with Python involves creating a seamless flow of information from various sources to their final storage destinations while data remains consistent, timely, and ready for analysis.

This process is crucial when handling large volumes of data efficiently, as maintaining its integrity throughout different stages is essential.

Data pipelines play an important role in modern data engineering, enabling organizations to harness valuable insights from their collected data.

This chapter aims to provide a comprehensive guide to constructing robust data pipelines tailored to diverse needs.

The upcoming chapter explains the fundamental components that constitute a data pipeline, emphasizing the origins of data, methods for ingesting it, processing techniques, and appropriate storage solutions.

You will gain insights into how data can originate from different sources, such as databases, APIs, and log files. In the process, you will also learn various data ingestion techniques suitable for both batch processing and real-time streaming.

Additionally, the chapter explores the importance of transforming raw data through cleaning and enrichment processes to ensure quality before loading it into suitable storage solutions like data warehouses or NoSQL databases.

We will also discuss practical implementation strategies for developing efficient ETL workflows using libraries such as Pandas and SQLAlchemy. We will highlight best practices for designing and automating these pipelines, equipping you with the knowledge to build scalable, resilient data architectures.

Components of a Data Pipeline

Understanding the Essential Components of a Data Pipeline

A data pipeline comprises several key components that work in unison to ensure the effective and efficient flow of data from one point to another.

These components include:

- the origins or sources of data.

- data ingestion techniques.

- processing methods.

- storage solutions.

Each of these elements plays a critical role in shaping a robust data pipeline.

Origins of Data: Databases, APIs, and Beyond

Data can originate from numerous sources, each contributing unique forms of information essential for various analyses and operations.

Common origins include:

- transactional databases, which store day-to-day business data.

- APIs (Application Programming Interfaces), which allow systems to communicate and share data in real-time.

- log files generated by applications and servers.

Additional sources could involve IoT (Internet of Things) devices recording sensor data and social media platforms generating user interaction data.

Understanding the diversity of data origins helps in designing pipelines that can efficiently gather and handle varied data types.

For example, a company might collect sales transaction data from its CRM system while simultaneously gathering user interaction data from its website analytics tool.

Combining these data points can provide comprehensive insights into customer behavior and preferences, facilitating more informed decision-making.

By recognizing the different origins of data, data engineers can design pipelines that cater to specific analytical needs, thereby enhancing the overall functionality of data processing systems.

Data Ingestion Techniques

Once the origins are identified, the next step is data ingestion. This involves bringing data into the pipeline using various techniques. Batch processing and real-time streaming are two primary methods of data ingestion.

Batch processing involves collecting and processing data at scheduled intervals, making it suitable for scenarios where real-time analysis is not critical. Conversely, real-time streaming ingests and processes data as it is generated, enabling immediate insights and actions.

Selecting the appropriate ingestion method depends on the application's requirements. For instance, financial services might require real-time data ingestion to monitor transactions and detect fraudulent activities instantly.

In contrast, a retail business analyzing weekly sales trends might opt for batch processing to consolidate and process data periodically.

By understanding different ingestion techniques, you can choose the most efficient methods for their specific needs, ensuring smooth data flow within the pipeline.

Guideline: When choosing a data ingestion technique, consider factors such as the required processing speed, data volume, and the criticality of real-time insights. This will help you select the optimal method.

Data Processing: Transforming Raw Data

After ingestion, the data often undergoes various processing steps to clean, enrich, and transform it into a format suitable for further analysis or storage.

Processing may involve:

- filtering out irrelevant data.

- aggregating information.

- handling missing values.

- performing complex computations.

For example, raw transactional data might be cleaned by removing duplicates and then enriched with additional contextual information, such as customer demographics.

Processing techniques can significantly impact the efficiency of data workflows. Using efficient algorithms and leveraging parallel processing can reduce the time required to transform large datasets.

Moreover, employing automated tools and frameworks can streamline the processing phase, minimizing manual intervention and potential errors.

Exposure to common processing techniques will help design effective workflows that ensure data quality and readiness for subsequent stages.

Guideline: Implement automated data validation checks during processing to ensure data integrity and consistency. This helps in maintaining high data quality across all pipeline stages.

Storage Solutions: Selecting the Right Destinations

The final stage in a data pipeline involves storing the processed data in an appropriate destination. Various storage solutions exist, each catering to specific needs.

- Data warehouses are optimized for structured data and complex queries, making them suitable for business intelligence and reporting applications.

- On the other hand, data lakes can store vast amounts of raw, unstructured data, offering flexibility for different analytical use cases.

NoSQL databases provide scalable storage for semi-structured and unstructured data. These are ideal for web applications requiring high availability and performance. Choosing the right storage solution depends on factors such as:

- data structure.

- access patterns.

- scalability requirements.

For instance, an e-commerce platform analyzing customer purchase history might use a data warehouse to enable fast and efficient querying of structured data.

Comprehending the various storage solutions empowers you to select the most suitable destinations for your data, optimizing storage costs and ensuring quick access to valuable insights.

Guideline: Regularly review storage performance and scalability to ensure the chosen solution continues to meet organizational needs as data volumes grow.

Implementing ETL Processes in Python

Implementing ETL processes in Python is essential for constructing efficient data pipelines that handle large volumes of data.

This subpoint explores the practical aspects of:

- building ETL (Extract, Transform, Load) workflows.

- focusing on using libraries like Pandas and Requests for data import.

- data cleaning and normalization strategies.

- options for loading data into various storage systems.

- automation techniques to streamline recurring tasks.

Extract

Python's versatility makes it an ideal choice for ETL operations. To start with, let's discuss how to import data seamlessly using libraries such as Pandas and Requests.

Pandas, renowned for its data manipulation capabilities, provides functions to read data from numerous sources, including:

- CSV files.

- Excel spreadsheets.

- SQL databases.

- web APIs.

For example, the pd.read_csv() function allows users to effortlessly import data from a CSV file into a Pandas DataFrame, establishing a structured format ideal for subsequent transformations.

Similarly, the Requests library facilitates fetching data from web APIs through simple HTTP requests, enabling data imports from online resources.

By leveraging these libraries, you can efficiently extract data from multiple sources, forming the foundation of your ETL processes.

Transform

Once data is extracted, the next step is to transform it, ensuring it meets quality standards and suits the intended analysis or application.

Data cleaning and normalization are critical to this stage, addressing common pitfalls in data quality. Cleaning involves identifying and rectifying inaccuracies or inconsistencies, such as:

- missing values.

- duplicates.

- incorrect data types.

Pandas provide robust tools for these tasks. The dropna() function removes rows or columns with missing data while fillna() replacing them with specified values, preserving the dataset's integrity.

Normalization, on the other hand, brings data into a uniform format or scale. Functions like astype() in Pandas help convert data types consistently, whereas the normalize() function scales numerical data, making it comparable across different units.

Implementing these techniques ensures the transformed data is accurate and consistent, ready for analysis or further processing.

Load

Loading data effectively into various storage systems forms the final step of the ETL process. Here, Python's flexibility shines, supporting integration with both SQL and NoSQL databases.

For SQL databases, libraries like SQLAlchemy enable seamless connections and interactions. Users can define database schemas, execute SQL queries, and load transformed data into tables using simple, intuitive commands.

Here's a basic example: after transforming your data with Pandas, you can use SQLAlchemy to establish a connection and load the data into an SQL table with the .to_sql() method.

ETL for NoSQL

For NoSQL databases, Python offers several libraries tailored to specific systems. MongoDB, a popular NoSQL database, integrates well with the PyMongo library, allowing for easy insertion of documents into collections.

Here, transformed data can be loaded into a MongoDB collection using simple syntax similar to SQLAlchemy. These examples highlight how Python's ecosystem accommodates diverse storage requirements, empowering data engineers to choose the optimal solution for their specific needs.

ETL Automation

Automation is pivotal in streamlining ETL processes, particularly for recurring tasks. Python supports various libraries designed to automate workflows, reducing manual intervention and enhancing efficiency.

Apache Airflow, for instance, excels in workflow automation by treating workflows as Directed Acyclic Graphs (DAGs). Users can define tasks and set dependencies, enabling automated execution and monitoring of complex ETL processes.

Additionally, Cron jobs, available directly in Unix-based systems, allow scheduling Python scripts to run at predetermined times, automating routine data extraction, transformation, and loading tasks.

By implementing automation techniques, data engineers can ensure their ETL pipelines run smoothly and reliably, conserving time and resources for more intricate data tasks.

One scenario that you could face as a data engineer is that you may need to build an ETL pipeline to analyze sales data from an e-commerce platform that sells merchandise like t-shirts.

When faced with such a scenario, you may use a Python script such as the one below. It provides a way to build and automate an ETL (Extract, Transform, Load) pipeline for analyzing sales data from an e-commerce platform.

Use the environment you have set up to follow the steps below and view the outcome that the script provides.

Python Script to Build and Automate an ETL Pipeline

```python
import pandas as pd
import sqlite3
from sqlalchemy import create_engine


# Step 1: Extract Data
def extract_data(file_path):
    data = pd.read_csv(file_path)
    return data


# Step 2: Transform Data
def transform_data(data):
    # Example transformation: filter out incomplete records
    cleaned_data = data.dropna()

    # Example transformation: convert date strings to datetime
objects
    cleaned_data['order_date'] =
pd.to_datetime(cleaned_data['order_date'])

    # Additional transformation logic can be added here
```

```python
        return cleaned_data


# Step 3: Load Data
def load_data(data, db_file):
    engine = create_engine(f'sqlite:///{db_file}')
    data.to_sql('sales_data', con=engine, if_exists='replace',
index=False)


# Main function to run the ETL pipeline
def run_etl(file_path, db_file):
    # Extract
    print("Extracting data...")
    data = extract_data(file_path)

    # Transform
    print("Transforming data...")
    transformed_data = transform_data(data)

    # Load
    print("Loading data into database...")
    load_data(transformed_data, db_file)

    print("ETL process completed successfully!")


# Example usage
if __name__ == "__main__":
    sales_data_file = 'sales_data.csv'  # Replace with your sales
data file path
    database_file = 'sales_data.db'     # Replace with your
desired database file path
    run_etl(sales_data_file, database_file)
```

Instructions:

1. Save the script in a Python file (e.g., etl_pipeline.py).

2. Make sure you have the necessary libraries installed by running:

```
pip install pandas sqlalchemy
```

3. Replace 'sales_data.csv' with the actual path to your sales data CSV file.

4. Run the script. It will extract the data, transform it by cleaning and formatting, and load it into a SQLite database.

You can extend the transformation logic based on your specific requirements.

As an alternative to using the script above, you could use the Requests library to fetch daily sales data via the platform's API. To do so, you will need to have the requests library installed. This is done by running the command

```
pip install requests
```

Thereafter,

```
import requests

daily_data = requests.get('http://sales-data-url.com')
```

will extract data from the server that contains the sales data(sales-data-url) and save it in the 'daily_data' variable.

Following extraction, you can employ Pandas to clean and normalize the data by filling in missing values, correcting data types, removing duplicates, and scaling numerical fields. One way of doing this is to use the following script:

Using Pandas to clean data from a dataset stored in the daily_data variable:

```python
import pandas as pd

# Assuming daily_data is defined and contains the dataset
# daily_data = your_data_here

# Convert daily_data to a DataFrame if it's not already
df = pd.DataFrame(daily_data)

# 1. Remove duplicates
df = df.drop_duplicates()

# 2. Handle missing values
# Option 1: Remove rows with missing values
df = df.dropna()

# Option 2: Fill missing values with a specific value (e.g., 0)
# df = df.fillna(0)

# 3. Rename columns (example: change 'old_name' to 'new_name')
# df.rename(columns={'old_name': 'new_name'}, inplace=True)

# 4. Convert data types (example: converting 'date' column to
datetime)
# df['date'] = pd.to_datetime(df['date'])

# 5. Filter out invalid data (example: removing rows where 'value'
< 0)
# df = df[df['value'] >= 0]

# Display the cleaned DataFrame
```

```
print(df)
```

Make sure to customize the script based on the specific cleaning requirements and the structure of your dataset.

Once the data is polished, you can load it into an SQL database using SQLAlchemy, organizing it into structured tables for analytical queries.

To ensure this process runs daily without manual effort, they can automate it using Apache Airflow, defining tasks and scheduling the workflow through DAGs.

This practical approach showcases how Python and its libraries facilitate efficient ETL operations, from data extraction to automated processing.

To help you with the process of creating an automated data pipeline, you can refer to the below script for guidance.

Test the script and the outcome created. This will provide you with a reference point and a level of comfort in knowing how to achieve this aspect of the task.

A Python script that uses Apache Airflow to create an automated data pipeline.

This script sets up a DAG (Directed Acyclic Graph) that defines the tasks and in what order they should run.

```python
from airflow import DAG
from airflow.operators.dummy_operator import DummyOperator
from airflow.operators.python_operator import PythonOperator
from datetime import datetime, timedelta

# Define the default_args dictionary
default_args = {
    'owner': 'airflow',
```

```python
    'depends_on_past': False,
    'start_date': datetime(2023, 1, 1),
    'email_on_failure': False,
    'email_on_retry': False,
    'retries': 1,
    'retry_delay': timedelta(minutes=5)
}


# Initialize the DAG
dag = DAG(
    'automated_data_pipeline',
    default_args=default_args,
    description='A simple automated data pipeline using Airflow',
    schedule_interval=timedelta(days=1)
)


# Define the Python function that will be called in the task
def extract():
    # Code to extract data from a source
    print("Extracting data...")


def transform():
    # Code to transform the data
    print("Transforming data...")


def load():
    # Code to load data to a destination
    print("Loading data...")


# Define the tasks
start = DummyOperator(task_id='start', dag=dag)


extract_task = PythonOperator(
```

```
    task_id='extract',
    python_callable=extract,
    dag=dag
)

transform_task = PythonOperator(
    task_id='transform',
    python_callable=transform,
    dag=dag
)

load_task = PythonOperator(
    task_id='load',
    python_callable=load,
    dag=dag
)

end = DummyOperator(task_id='end', dag=dag)

# Set the task dependencies
start >> extract_task >> transform_task >> load_task >> end
```

This script consists of the following parts:

- Importing necessary modules and classes from Airflow.

- Setting default arguments for the DAG (such as the start date and retry settings).

- Creating a new DAG with the specified schedule.

- Defining three simple tasks: extract, transform, and load, which would contain the actual logic for data extraction, transformation, and loading.

- Creating dependencies between tasks using the bitwise shift operator (>>).

Make sure to customize the functions and logic to suit your specific data pipeline requirements.

Handling Real-Time Data Streaming

When dealing with real-time data streaming, it is crucial to understand that this approach differs significantly from traditional ETL (extract, transform, load) processes.

Traditional ETL systems operate in batch mode, where large volumes of data are processed and then loaded at set intervals, leading to higher latency.

In contrast, real-time data streaming ensures continuous input, processing, and output of data with minimal delay, making it ideal for scenarios requiring immediate insights and actions.

The first step in managing real-time data streaming effectively involves recognizing potential real-time data sources. These include IoT (Internet of Things) devices that send continuous streams of sensor data, user activity feeds from websites or mobile apps, financial transaction records, and social media updates.

By identifying these sources, you can set up a data pipeline that captures and processes this data seamlessly as it arrives.

To handle the influx of real-time data, various frameworks have been developed, each suited for different use cases and requirements. Two popular choices are Apache Kafka and Apache Flink.

Apache Kafka

Apache Kafka is widely used for building real-time data pipelines and streaming applications due to its high throughput, fault tolerance, and scalability.

It works by ingesting data streams into topic-based partitions, which can be consumed by multiple downstream applications simultaneously.

This makes Kafka an excellent choice for scenarios requiring reliable message delivery and stream processing integration (Pucariello, 2024).

Apache Flink

On the other hand, Apache Flink excels in complex event processing and real-time analytics due to its advanced capabilities in stateful computations.

Unlike Kafka, which primarily focuses on message streaming, Flink is designed to handle both stream and batch processing within a single framework.

This versatility allows for more sophisticated real-time data analysis, making it suitable for applications such as anomaly detection, real-time decision-making, and continuous ETL processes.

Flink's ability to support stateful operations means it can keep track of data states across events, enabling easier implementation of windowing, time-based operations, and event-time processing (RisingWave, 2024).

Windowing

Understanding the concept of windowing is essential when working with real-time data streams. Windowing allows you to break down infinite data streams into manageable chunks based on time intervals or event counts.

This segmentation is crucial for performing timely analysis and aggregations. For instance, you might want to calculate the average sensor reading over the last minute or detect spikes in user activity within a five-minute window.

Both Kafka Streams and Flink offer robust support for windowing, but they differ in their implementations.

- Flink provides features like session windows and custom window functions.

- Kafka Streams offers simpler APIs that integrate seamlessly with Apache Kafka topics.

Therefore, when selecting which option to use, start by deciding which windowing method best suits your needs.

Partitioning

Real-time data streaming also requires efficient load balancing techniques to manage high throughput scenarios.

As data volume increases, it is vital to distribute the processing load evenly across multiple nodes or instances to prevent bottlenecks and ensure continued performance.

One common technique is partitioning, which divides the data stream into smaller, more manageable segments that can be processed in parallel.

Both Kafka and Flink support partitioning, but they handle it differently (RisingWave, 2024).

- In Kafka, data is partitioned based on keys assigned to each message, ensuring that all messages with the same key are sent to the same partition. This guarantees ordering while allowing horizontal scaling.

- Apache Flink, meanwhile, uses keyed state management, distributing data based on keys across operators rather than partitions. This approach facilitates efficient state handling and dynamic scaling, adapting to changes in data volume or processing needs without significant downtime or reconfiguration.

Developing skills to manage real-time data streams effectively entails a good understanding of the tools and methods mentioned above.

Proficiency in setting up and configuring Kafka and Flink environments is crucial. Knowledge of programming languages like Java, Scala, or Python, often used with these frameworks, is also important.

Understanding how to implement and manage windowing strategies, stateful operations, and load balancing techniques forms the backbone of effective real-time data stream management.

Final Thoughts

This chapter has explored the key components necessary for building efficient data pipelines. We began by understanding various data origins, including databases, APIs, and IoT devices, which form the foundation of any pipeline.

Next, we delved into different data ingestion techniques, such as batch processing and real-time streaming. These methods are crucial in determining how data enters the system based on specific requirements.

We also examined the critical processing steps to transform raw data into a usable format, using cleaning and enrichment strategies to maintain data quality.

Finally, we discussed various storage solutions, emphasizing the importance of selecting appropriate destinations tailored to the data's structure and access needs.

Actionable guidelines were provided throughout the chapter to ensure that each step of building a data pipeline is executed efficiently.

These insights will equip you with the knowledge to design robust pipelines capable of handling large datasets while maintaining high performance and reliability.

From identifying diverse data sources to leveraging Python libraries for ETL processes and managing real-time data streaming, you will find yourself well-prepared to implement best practices in your data engineering projects.

This comprehensive approach ensures that you can optimize your data workflows, making informed decisions that enhance both the functionality and scalability of your systems.

After knowing how to load the data onto the system, you will need to find ways to effectively manipulate it in different ways. Understanding practical algorithms that can help you in this step is the subject of the next chapter.

CHAPTER 7

Practical Algorithms for Data Applications

Implementing practical algorithms is essential for solving real-world problems in data applications. This chapter provides you with the necessary skills and understanding to build efficient data systems using Python. By focusing on concrete examples and clear explanations, we aim to equip you with tools you can apply directly to your work. The emphasis will be on how these algorithms can be leveraged to handle various data tasks effectively.

You will explore a range of fundamental algorithms crucial for data organization and retrieval. We start by exploring sorting algorithms such as Bubble Sort, Quick Sort, and Merge Sort, highlighting their significance and efficiency in managing large datasets.

Following this, we delve into search algorithms—linear and binary searches—to illustrate their role in efficient data retrieval. The chapter also covers performance and complexity analysis, introducing Big O notation to help understand the scalability of these algorithms.

Real-world case studies, such as optimizing database queries and enhancing web application performance, will demonstrate the practical applications of these concepts. By the end of this chapter, readers will have a solid grounding in implementing key algorithms and an appreciation for their impact on data-intensive tasks.

Sorting and Searching Algorithms

In this section, we'll delve into fundamental algorithms that are pivotal for organizing and retrieving data, providing you with the essential skills to manage large datasets effectively. Understanding these algorithms can significantly enhance one's ability to tackle complex data tasks efficiently.

We begin with an overview of basic sorting algorithms: Bubble Sort, Quick Sort, and Merge Sort. Sorting algorithms are crucial as they help in organizing data, making it easier to manage and search.

Bubble sort is a simple algorithm in which each pair of adjacent elements is compared, and the elements are swapped if they are in the wrong order. This process repeats until the entire list is sorted. Although easy to implement, Bubble Sort has high time complexity, $O(n^2)$, making it inefficient for large datasets.

Quick sort, on the other hand, is more efficient. It uses a divide-and-conquer approach where the array is divided into sub-arrays based on a pivot element; elements less than the pivot go to the left, while those greater go to the right.

These sub-arrays are then sorted recursively. Quick Sort has an average-case time complexity of $O(n \log n)$, but its worst-case performance is $O(n^2)$, which generally happens when the smallest or largest element is always chosen as the pivot. However, with random pivots or using the median as a pivot, this worst-case scenario can be mitigated, making Quick Sort very efficient for most practical purposes.

Merge sort also employs a divide-and-conquer strategy but works by splitting the array into halves, sorting each half, and merging them back together. Unlike Quick Sort, Merge Sort consistently has a time complexity of $O(n \log n)$ regardless of the initial order of elements.

Its drawback lies in space complexity, $O(n)$, as it requires additional storage proportional to the input size. Merge Sort is particularly useful when stability (preserving the relative order of equal elements) is required and in situations involving large datasets that fit external storage needs.

Next, we introduce linear and binary search algorithms, highlighting their efficiency in data retrieval. Linear search is the simplest search algorithm where each element in a list is checked sequentially until the target value is found or the list ends. Its time complexity is $O(n)$, making it inefficient for large datasets.

However, linear search is useful when dealing with unsorted data or small lists where the overhead of advanced searching methods does not justify their use.

Binary search is far more efficient but requires a sorted list. It works by repeatedly dividing the search interval in half. If the target value is equal to the middle element, the search ends. If the target value is smaller, the search continues on the lower half; if larger, on the upper half.

Binary search has a time complexity of $O(\log n)$, making it ideal for large sorted datasets, significantly reducing the number of comparisons needed to find the target value.

Understanding the performance and complexity of sorting and searching algorithms is critical, which is where Big O notation comes into play. Big O notation allows us to describe the upper bound or worst-case scenario of an algorithm's runtime complexity based on input size. It abstracts away constant factors and lower-order terms, focusing on dominant terms that determine scalability.

Big O notation is vital for several reasons. First, it provides a high-level analysis of an algorithm's performance without getting bogged down in implementation details. Emphasizing the dominant term helps developers understand how the runtime scales with input size, aiding in selecting the most efficient algorithm for a given problem. Further, it facilitates comparative analysis, enabling developers to compare different algorithms' complexities and choose the best one accordingly.

For instance, comparing Quick Sort ($O(n \log n)$) with Bubble Sort ($O(n^2)$), it's evident that Quick Sort will handle larger datasets more efficiently. Understanding Big O also aids in predicting an algorithm's scalability, which is crucial for designing systems expected to handle varying loads efficiently. Moreover, in software development, knowledge of Big O guides optimization efforts by identifying potential bottlenecks.

Real World Applicability

Real-world applications demonstrate the indispensability of these algorithms in data-intensive scenarios. Consider a database system requiring quick data retrieval.

Utilizing Binary Search over a sorted index can drastically reduce query times compared to a linear search. In another case, web applications often need to sort massive user data; implementing Merge Sort or Quick Sort can optimize this process considerably.

E-Commerce

Let's explore a few practical case studies to solidify our understanding. The first scenario involves an e-commerce platform handling millions of product listings. Implementing Quick Sort enables rapid price sorting, enhancing user experience as customers filter products. Here, the efficiency of Quick Sort ensures minimal delay even with extensive stock data.

Search Engines

In another scenario, consider a search engine. The necessity to quickly retrieve relevant search results from an immense database cannot rely on linear search due to its inefficiency. Instead, binary search algorithms over pre-sorted indices ensure fast, accurate search result delivery, improving response times and user satisfaction.

Scientific Computing

Furthermore, in scientific computing, vast datasets like genomic data are continuously managed and manipulated. Efficient sorting algorithms like Merge Sort facilitate organizing this data for subsequent analysis, ensuring consistency and reliability.

Graph Algorithms for Network Data

To introduce graph-theoretic concepts and algorithms essential for handling network data, we begin with an overview of graph terminology and structures. Graphs are mathematical representations consisting of nodes (vertices) connected by edges (links).

Nodes represent entities such as people or locations, and edges denote relationships between these entities. Weights can be added to edges to indicate the strength or capacity of connections. Fundamental elements include paths (sequences of edges connecting nodes) and cycles (paths that start and end at the same node).

Graphs are categorized based on various characteristics:

- directed vs. undirected (whether edges have a direction)

- weighted vs. unweighted (whether edges have associated values)

- cyclic vs. acyclic (whether cycles exist within the graph)

- bipartite (nodes divided into two distinct sets)

- temporal (connections change over time)

Understanding these basic terminologies provides a foundation for exploring more advanced concepts and applications.

Essential graph algorithms prove invaluable in solving real-world problems. Among these, **Dijkstra's algorithm** is fundamental for finding the shortest path between nodes in a graph.

It operates by systematically selecting the node with the smallest known distance from the starting point and updating the distances of its neighbors. Python implementations typically use libraries like NetworkX. For instance, to find the shortest path using NetworkX, one might write:

```python
import networkx as nx

G = nx.Graph()
G.add_weighted_edges_from([(1, 2, 4), (1, 3, 2), (2, 3, 5),
(2, 4, 10), (3, 4, 3)])
shortest_path = nx.dijkstra_path(G, source=1, target=4)
print(shortest_path)
```

Depth-first search (DFS) is another critical algorithm used primarily for traversing or searching tree or graph data structures. DFS starts at the root node and explores as far as possible along each branch before backtracking. This method is particularly useful for detecting cycles and performing pathfinding in scenarios where all nodes need to be visited. A simple Python implementation might look like this:

```python
def dfs(graph, start, visited=None):
    if visited is None:
        visited = set()
    visited.add(start)
    print(start)

    for next_node in graph[start]:
        if next_node not in visited:
            dfs(graph, next_node, visited)

graph = {
    'A': ['B', 'C'],
    'B': ['D', 'E'],
    'C': ['F'],
    'D': [],
    'E': ['F'],
    'F': []
}
dfs(graph, 'A')
```

Practical use cases of these graph algorithms abound. In social networks, graphs model relationships among users, allowing the identification of key influencers or community clusters.

Transportation systems leverage shortest-path algorithms to optimize routing and reduce travel times.

Recommendation systems utilize graph theory to enhance recommendation accuracy by analyzing user-item interactions and predicting potential interests based on graph traversal techniques.

For example, a recommendation system might use collaborative filtering by constructing a bipartite graph linking users and items.

Implementing this in Python could involve creating a graph where user nodes connect to item nodes they've interacted with. By traversing this graph, the system can recommend items to users based on the preferences of similar users.

To solidify your understanding, try the following coding challenge that focuses on graph algorithms. Implement a function that detects whether a given graph is connected (i.e., there is a path between every pair of nodes). Here is the starting point for the challenge:

```python
def is_connected(graph):
    visited = set()

    def dfs(node):
        if node not in visited:
            visited.add(node)
            for neighbor in graph[node]:
                dfs(neighbor)

    start_node = list(graph.keys())[0]
    dfs(start_node)

    return len(visited) == len(graph)

graph = {
    'A': ['B', 'C'],
    'B': ['A', 'D', 'E'],
    'C': ['A', 'F'],
    'D': ['B'],
```

```
    'E': ['B', 'F'],
    'F': ['C', 'E']
  }
print(is_connected(graph))
```

Another exercise you can engage in involves building a graph representing a social network.

Once you have built the graph illustrated above, apply BFS (Breadth-First Search) and DFS to identify communities or influential users. This will provide you with practical insights into your data.

When you incorporate these case studies and engage in coding exercises, you can intuitively grasp the significance of graph-theoretic algorithms.

Mastering these concepts and tools will significantly expand your capabilities in handling data-intensive applications effectively, whether optimizing supply chains, modeling biological networks, or enhancing recommender systems.

Machine Learning Basics With scikit-learn

Machine learning is a pivotal part of modern data science, lending its power to a wide range of applications, from predictive analytics to autonomous systems.

Understanding the core concepts of machine learning and practical implementations using libraries like scikit-learn can empower you to make data-driven decisions.

This section introduces fundamental machine learning principles and provides hands-on guidance for setting up scikit-learn in Python.

To start with, machine learning encompasses three primary types: supervised learning, unsupervised learning, and reinforcement learning.

Supervised learning involves learning a function that maps an input to an output based on example input-output pairs. It's commonly used when we have labeled data—data paired with correct answers—such as predicting house prices based on features like size, location, and number of bedrooms (Afzal Badshah, PhD, 2024).

Unsupervised learning, on the other hand, deals with unlabeled data. The goal here is to identify hidden patterns or intrinsic structures in input data.

Clustering algorithms, such as k-means, fall under this category and are used for tasks like customer segmentation, which aims to group customers into different segments based on their buying behavior.

Reinforcement learning is distinct from the previous two types. It revolves around an agent that learns to make decisions by performing actions in an environment to maximize cumulative reward.

This type of learning is often used in areas requiring sequential decision-making, such as robotics, gaming, and navigation systems (<i>Python Machine Learning: Scikit-Learn Tutorial</i>, n.d.). Together, these paradigms lay the foundation for understanding how different machine learning models operate and adapt to various problem domains.

Installing Scikit-learn

With a grounding in these core concepts, the next step is to get started with scikit-learn, a powerful and user-friendly Python library for implementing machine learning models. Installing scikit-learn is straightforward. You can do it via pip, the package installer for Python:

```
pip install -U scikit-learn
```

Once installed, you'll want to familiarize yourself with some basic functionalities through simple coding examples. The library includes modules for both supervised and unsupervised learning, along with tools for model selection and evaluation. To demonstrate, let's walk through a basic workflow of loading data, training a model, and making predictions.

First, load one of scikit-learn's built-in datasets:

```
from sklearn.datasets import load_wine
wine_data = load_wine()
X, y = wine_data.data, wine_data.target
```

Here, X contains the input features and y holds the target labels. Next, split the dataset into training and testing sets to evaluate the model's performance on unseen data:

```
from     sklearn.model_selection     import     train_test_split
X_train, X_test, y_train, y_test = train_test_split(X, y,
test_size=0.3, random_state=42)
```

Now, to introduce you to a simple algorithm, we'll implement a linear regression model. Linear regression aims to model the relationship between a dependent variable and one or more independent variables by fitting a linear equation. Begin by importing and initializing the model:

```
from sklearn.linear_model import LinearRegression
model = LinearRegression()
```

Train the model using the training data:

```
model.fit(X_train, y_train)
```

After training, use the model to make predictions on the test set:

```
y_pred = model.predict(X_test)
```

Following predictions, it's crucial to assess the model's performance using key metrics like accuracy, precision, and recall. These metrics provide insight into how well the model generalizes to new data.

Accuracy measures the proportion of correct predictions out of the total number of predictions. Precision tells us the proportion of true positive predictions among all positive predictions, while recall indicates the proportion of true positive predictions out of the actual positives:

```
from sklearn.metrics import mean_squared_error, r2_score

# Calculate performance metrics
mse = mean_squared_error(y_test, y_pred)
r2 = r2_score(y_test, y_pred)

print(f'Mean Squared Error: {mse}')
print(f'R² Score: {r2}')
```

Mean Squared Error (MSE) measures the average squared difference between the observed actual outcomes and the outcomes predicted by the model. A lower MSE indicates a better fit. The R_2 score, also known as the coefficient of determination, ranges from 0 to 1, with 1 indicating perfect prediction.

The described steps offer a tangible introduction to building and evaluating a machine learning model using scikit-learn. By understanding the principles of supervised, unsupervised, and reinforcement learning, setting up scikit-learn, and working through an example of linear regression, you can begin your journey into the realm of data-driven decision-making.

Bringing It All Together

In this chapter, we explored various sorting and searching algorithms like Bubble Sort, Quick Sort, Merge Sort, Linear Search, and Binary Search. These fundamental techniques are critical for organizing and retrieving data efficiently, which is essential in many real-world applications.

We also discussed the importance of understanding algorithmic complexity using Big O notation, allowing you to compare different methods and select the most efficient ones for your specific needs.

By mastering these algorithms, you will be equipped with practical skills that enhance your ability to manage large datasets and build efficient data systems using Python. This knowledge is invaluable for anyone looking to optimize performance in data-intensive scenarios, from database management to search engines and recommendation systems.

As you continue your journey, keep experimenting with these algorithms and applying them to different problems to deepen your understanding and proficiency. In the next chapter, we will explore advanced topics like microservices, event-driven architecture, the implementation of restful APIs, and security considerations. Knowledge and mastery of these areas will help you further hone your skills.

CHAPTER 8

Advanced Topics in System Design

Exploring advanced topics in system design is key to building and maintaining complex, data-intensive applications.

These applications require robust architectures, efficient programming paradigms, reliable API implementations, and stringent security measures to ensure functionality and performance at scale.

This chapter outlines the concepts essential for modern software engineers and data professionals who aim to push the boundaries of what their systems can achieve.

This chapter introduces you to a variety of architectural patterns, such as microservices and event-driven programming.

The discussion extends to implementation techniques with RESTful APIs, highlighting best practices in construction, security, and performance optimization. You will also gain insights into programming paradigms that support scalable and maintainable systems and thoroughly explorepromptly diagnosing issues security protocols essential to safeguarding data.

This comprehensive overview aims to equip you with the knowledge and tools necessary to excel in designing high-performing, resilient systems in today's demanding tech landscape.

Microservices Architecture

Microservices architecture represents a significant shift in the way data-intensive applications are designed and maintained.

Unlike traditional monolithic applications, where all components are interconnected and interdependent, microservices break down functionalities into smaller, independent services. This modularity has profound implications for enhancing agility, maintainability, and overall system resilience.

Agility

One of the primary benefits of microservices is agility. By allowing each service to be developed, deployed, and scaled independently, teams can release updates and features faster without waiting for the entire application to be redeployed.

This independent deployment capability means that development teams can work on different services simultaneously, thereby significantly speeding up the development process and fostering innovation. Additionally, this approach reduces downtime, as updates to one service do not necessitate taking the whole application offline.

Autonomy

Moreover, microservices architecture enhances team autonomy. Each team can manage its own service independently, choosing the best tools and technologies suited to its specific needs without having to worry about synchronizing with other teams.

This independence leads to greater parallelization of efforts and minimizes bottlenecks often encountered in monolithic structures. Consequently, teams can apply their expertise more effectively to solve domain-specific challenges, leading to higher-quality outputs and more satisfied developers.

Mitigating Failures

Equally important is how microservices mitigate the impact of failures. In a monolithic application, a failure in one component can potentially bring down the entire system.

However, within a microservices framework, an issue in one service is isolated and does not necessarily affect the functioning of other services.

This containment of faults ensures that applications remain robust and available even when individual components face issues. It also simplifies troubleshooting and maintenance by focusing on the failing service without sifting through an extensive codebase.

Implementation

Several design patterns have emerged to support the effective implementation of microservices. The API Gateway pattern is one of the most commonly used.

API Gateways

An API Gateway acts as a single entry point for client requests, routing them to appropriate microservices.

This centralization simplifies interaction with the backend systems by offloading tasks such as authentication, request routing, and load balancing to the gateway.

For instance, Netflix uses Zuul as its API Gateway, handling over a billion API calls daily. This enables seamless integration and efficient communication between clients and services.

Command Query Responsibility Segregation

Another notable pattern is the Command Query Responsibility Segregation (CQRS). CQRS separates the read and write operations into distinct models, allowing each to be optimized and scaled independently.

This separation reduces contention between read and write processes, enhancing performance and scalability. For example, in an e-commerce application, CQRS might be used to maintain separate databases for handling transactional queries and analytical queries.

This differentiation not only improves performance but also provides a clear structure for handling complex business logic.

Saga Pattern

The Saga pattern is particularly useful when managing distributed transactions across multiple services. Unlike in monolithic systems, where transactions are managed centrally, microservices must handle transactions that span several services.

The Saga pattern breaks down a large transaction into smaller steps, each managed by a different service. If one step fails, compensating transactions are triggered to undo the previous steps, ensuring data consistency.

A classic example is a travel booking system involving flight, hotel, and car rental services. Each service completes its part of the booking, and if any part fails, the steps taken by other services are undone to maintain consistency.

Addressing Data Consistency Needs

Implementing microservices presents challenges, particularly in maintaining data consistency.

Ensuring that data remains consistent across distributed services can be complex, given the asynchronous nature of operations.

Synchronous communication between services can lead to tight coupling, defeating the purpose of microservices. Hence, implementing effective orchestration tools becomes crucial. These tools help coordinate service interactions and manage dependencies efficiently.

Kubernetes

Kubernetes, for instance, provides container orchestration capabilities that simplify the deployment, scaling, and management of containerized applications.

Logging and Monitoring

Logging and monitoring are equally critical in a microservices environment due to the distributed nature of the architecture. Each service generates logs independently, making it challenging to track and correlate events across the entire system.

Therefore, robust logging frameworks and centralized log management solutions like ELK Stack (Elasticsearch, Logstash, Kibana) or Prometheus with Grafana are indispensable.

These tools provide visibility into the application's health, facilitate real-time monitoring and aid in promptly diagnosing issues.

Microservices in the Real World

The real-world adoption of microservices showcases its transformative impact. Companies like Amazon, Netflix, and Uber have successfully transitioned from monolithic architectures to microservices. Amazon, for example, moved to microservices to handle the massive scale and complexity of its e-commerce platform.

By breaking down its monolithic application into hundreds of microservices, Amazon could innovate faster, improve fault isolation, and scale its services independently.

Similarly, Uber's shift to a microservices architecture enabled it to support rapid growth and introduce new features swiftly. Each service, from ride-hailing to payments, operates independently, allowing Uber to iterate and expand its offerings without disrupting existing functionalities.

Event-Driven Programming and Message Queues

Event-driven programming has become a cornerstone in the design of responsive, data-intensive systems. By focusing on events that trigger actions rather than traditional request-response methods, this architecture fundamentally enhances how applications manage and respond to vast amounts of data in real-time scenarios.

At the heart of event-driven systems is the decoupling of event producers from consumers. This separation allows each component to function independently, which not only boosts scalability but also facilitates seamless integration across diverse services.

For example, in an online retail platform, an order placement might trigger inventory updates, shipping notifications, and customer alerts as independent events. Each of these actions happens asynchronously, allowing for a more fluid and responsive system.

Message Queues

A pivotal element in achieving this asynchronous processing is the use of message queues. These queues serve as intermediaries that buffer messages between producers and consumers.

By doing so, they handle spikes in data traffic gracefully, ensuring that no message is lost even if the receiving component is temporarily down or overloaded.

Tools such as RabbitMQ and Apache Kafka are widely employed in high-volume environments due to their robustness and efficiency. These technologies ensure message reliability and persistence, which are crucial for maintaining consistent operations.

Idempotency

Designing effective event-driven systems requires adherence to several key principles. One critical principle is emphasizing idempotency, which guarantees that processing the same event multiple times will produce the same result.

This is vital in scenarios where network issues or duplicate messages might otherwise cause inconsistent states. Idempotency ensures that operations like updating user records or processing payments remain stable and reliable despite potential disruptions.

Event Sourcing

Another essential concept is event sourcing, which involves storing all state-changing events as a sequence of immutable records. This approach not only improves auditability and accountability but also provides an accurate historical representation of the system's state over time.

Event sourcing enables replay capabilities, where past events can be reprocessed to reconstruct the system's state. This significantly aids the debugging and testing processes.

Mitigating Message Loss

However, implementing event-driven architectures is not without its challenges. One significant hurdle is handling message loss, which occurs when messages fail to reach their intended consumers. Implementing mechanisms such as acknowledgments and retries can mitigate this issue but require careful planning and robust infrastructure.

Another challenge is ensuring the correct processing order of events. In distributed systems where events may arrive out of order, leveraging techniques like sequence numbering or using specialized data structures can help maintain the integrity of event sequences.

Designing fault-tolerant systems to handle unpredictable failures adds another layer of complexity. Redundancy and replication strategies are critical to ensure that the system can recover gracefully from failures.

Additionally, monitoring and observability tools are indispensable for identifying and diagnosing issues in real-time.

Implementing RESTful APIs

In the rapidly evolving landscape of system design, RESTful APIs have emerged as a critical component for ensuring the seamless interoperability of various system components. This subpoint delves into the significance of RESTful APIs and outlines their essential principles, construction using Python frameworks, security measures, and performance optimization techniques.

Principles of REST

REST (Representational State Transfer) is an architectural style that has become ubiquitous in the design of networked applications. At its core, REST operates on several key principles that promote simplicity, scalability, and adaptability in distributed systems.

Statelessness

One of these principles is statelessness, which means that each request from a client to a server must contain all the information needed to understand and process the request.

Servers do not store any client context between requests, which simplifies interactions and increases reliability. This stateless behavior allows for greater scalability as the server does not need to manage or store session state, thereby reducing overhead.

Using Uniform Resource Identifiers

Another fundamental principle of REST is the use of Uniform Resource Identifiers (URIs) to uniquely identify resources. Each resource in a RESTful system, such as a piece of data or service endpoint, can be accessed via a unique URI.

This clear identification method enhances the clarity and predictability of service interactions, making it easier for developers to construct and debug requests.

GET, POST, DELETE

REST also employs standard HTTP methods—GET for retrieving data, POST for creating resources, PUT for updating resources, and DELETE for removing resources. These methods are universally understood across different platforms, facilitating straightforward integration and interoperability.

By adhering to these methods, RESTful APIs ensure a consistent and comprehensible approach to performing operations on resources.

Building With Python

Python's versatile and robust ecosystem offers powerful frameworks like Flask and Django for developing RESTful APIs.

Flask

Flask is a lightweight micro-framework ideal for rapid API development. It allows developers to quickly set up routing and handle requests with minimal overhead. Flask's simplicity makes it an excellent choice for building smaller-scale APIs or prototyping new features.

Django

For more complex and large-scale API implementations, Django stands out due to its comprehensive suite of built-in features.

Unlike Flask, Django provides a more integrated environment with tools for database management, authentication, and templates required for developing intricate APIs. Both Flask and Django support versioning, which is crucial for maintaining backward compatibility as APIs evolve.

Additionally, extensive documentation ensures that APIs are easy to use and maintain, fostering better collaboration among development teams.

Securing APIs

Security is paramount when designing RESTful APIs, especially when dealing with sensitive data. One effective strategy is implementing OAuth (Open Authorization), which allows third-party applications to securely access user resources without exposing credentials.

OAuth works by providing tokens that grant access permissions, ensuring that user data remains protected even when interfaced with multiple services.

Stateless Authentication

Another method for securing APIs is using JSON Web Tokens (JWT) for stateless authentication. JWTs encapsulate claims about the user and are signed to verify their authenticity.

Since they are self-contained and stateless, JWTs enhance user experience by eliminating the need for the server to maintain session data, thus improving scalability.

Role-Based Access Control

Implementing access controls is equally vital. Access control mechanisms dictate who can view or manipulate specific resources within the system, ensuring that sensitive data is only accessible to authorized users.

These controls can be enforced through role-based access control (RBAC) or attribute-based access control (ABAC) systems. By clearly defining who has access to what data, robust security postures can be maintained across RESTful APIs.

Performance Optimization

Several strategies can be employed to ensure the optimal performance of RESTful APIs.

Rate Limiting

Rate limiting is a technique used to prevent abuse and ensure stability under heavy usage. By limiting the number of requests a client can make to an API endpoint within a given time frame, rate limiting protects the system from being overwhelmed by excessive traffic, thereby maintaining consistent performance levels.

Caching

Caching is another powerful optimization tool. By storing frequently accessed data in a cache, both server load and response times can be significantly reduced.

Cached responses enable quicker data retrieval since repeated requests can be served from the cache rather than reprocessed by the server each time. Implementing HTTP cache headers like ETag and Cache-Control directives inform clients and proxies about the cacheability of responses, further enhancing efficiency.

Security Audits

Regular security audits play a crucial role in identifying vulnerabilities within APIs. These audits involve systematically examining the API's codebase, configurations, and deployment environment to uncover potential security flaws or weaknesses.

Proactive auditing helps address issues before they can be exploited, thereby safeguarding the integrity and reliability of the API.

Final Thoughts

This chapter provided an in-depth examination of advanced concepts in system design crucial for developing complex data-intensive applications.

The discussion explored microservices architecture and highlighted its benefits in promoting agility, team autonomy, and fault tolerance.

Key patterns such as API Gateway, CQRS, and Saga were introduced to demonstrate effective microservice implementation. Moreover, the importance of logging, monitoring, and real-world examples illustrated the transformative impact of microservices on modern system design.

Event-driven programming was discussed as an essential approach for building responsive systems that handle vast amounts of data efficiently.

The use of message queues like RabbitMQ and Apache Kafka ensures reliable asynchronous communication between decoupled components. Principles like idempotency and event sourcing were emphasized to maintain consistency and reliability.

Finally, implementing RESTful APIs with a focus on principles, security measures, and performance optimization was covered, showcasing the role of APIs in ensuring seamless interoperability in distributed systems.

As you explore hands-on projects and case studies in the next chapter, keep these newly learned concepts in mind and identify opportunities for implementing each concept.

CHAPTER 9

Hands-On Projects and Case Studies

Hands-on projects and case studies provide a practical approach to mastering advanced concepts in designing data-intensive applications when using Python.

By immersing yourself in real-world examples, you will gain valuable insights into how theoretical principles translate into actual solutions. This chapter bridges the gap between understanding abstract ideas and applying them to tangible tasks, offering a robust framework for enhancing your data engineering skills.

Throughout this chapter, you will explore an array of hands-on projects that delve into complex areas such as building scalable systems, crafting sophisticated machine learning models, and deploying efficient data management processes.

Detailed case studies will illustrate the challenges faced by engineers in various industries and the innovative strategies they employ to overcome these hurdles.

These examples will not only demonstrate effective problem-solving techniques but also highlight best practices and lessons learned. This will equip you with the knowledge and tools necessary for tackling similar issues in your own projects.

Building a Scalable Recommendation System

Designing and implementing a scalable recommendation engine involves understanding several critical components that ensure efficiency, accuracy, and scalability. In this section, you will perform an in-depth exploration of essential techniques and methodologies for crafting such engines.

One of the fundamental aspects of a recommendation engine is its ability to capture and analyze user preferences effectively. Various algorithms can be used to achieve this goal, each with unique strengths.

Collaborative filtering maps the relationship between users and individual products in the database. The identified relationships are then used to suggest products. It to users.

This is one of the most popular approaches used in recommendation systems. It leverages the wisdom of the crowd to make predictions based on similarities between users or items. It can be implemented using user-based or item-based strategies, both of which have proven effective in different scenarios.

For instance, user-based collaborative filtering identifies users with similar tastes and recommends items they like, while item-based filtering suggests items similar to those the user has shown interest in.

Content-based filtering recommends items by comparing the attributes of items and users.

This is an analytical technique that relies heavily on the features of items and user profiles, making it suitable for environments with rich metadata. Hybrid approaches that combine collaborative and content-based filtering often yield better results by mitigating the limitations inherent in each method.

Capturing user preferences generates large datasets that need to be efficiently stored and managed. The choice between SQL and NoSQL databases plays a significant role in handling data storage needs. SQL databases offer structured query language support and are ideal for relational data models.

They ensure consistency and support complex queries but may struggle with horizontal scaling. NoSQL databases, on the other hand, provide flexibility with unstructured data and are designed for horizontal scalability.

They excel in high-velocity environments where schema evolution and distributed data processing are paramount.

Caching frequently accessed data reduces latency, providing users with quicker recommendations. Techniques like in-memory caching and distributed caches ensure that the system remains responsive even under heavy use (binhnguyennus, 2017).

Training machine learning models to power recommendation engines is the next critical step. The process starts with data preprocessing, where raw data is cleaned and transformed by removing duplicates and fixing errors.

This ensures quality input data is used for the models. Feature engineering is vital here, as it involves creating relevant features that capture the underlying patterns in the data. Domain knowledge plays a significant role in identifying valuable features that influence recommendation quality.

Algorithms For Training Models

Once the data is prepared, different algorithms like the ones described below can be employed to train models.

- Matrix factorization decomposes a matrix into the product of two or more simpler matrixes to reveal hidden patterns and relationships within the data.

- Neural networks consist of interconnected nodes (neurons) organized in layers. This enables them to learn and make predictions from data through a process of adjusting connection weights based on input-output mappings.

- Gradient boosting is an ensemble learning method that sequentially combines multiple weak predictive models, usually decision trees, to improve accuracy by minimizing the prediction error using gradient descent.

Model evaluation is crucial to ensure that performance meets expectations. Metrics like accuracy, precision, recall, and F1-score help measure the quality of recommendations.

Accuracy indicates the proportion of correct predictions, while precision and recall provide insights into the relevance and completeness of the recommendations, respectively.

F1-score provides a single metric that measures the accuracy of positive predictions and the identification of all relevant instances in a binary classification task.

A/B testing in production environments allows continuous improvement by comparing model performance under different conditions (Ignito, 2024). A/B testing is a statistical method used to compare two versions of a webpage, product, or marketing strategy by randomly assigning users to each version and measuring performance to determine which one is more effective.

Using version control for models is advisable to manage different iterations effectively. Tools like MLflow or DVC can track changes in model parameters and configurations, ensuring reproducibility and facilitating rollbacks if necessary.

Effective deployment methods are essential for real-time recommendation systems. Employing a microservices architecture enables the decomposition of the recommendation engine into smaller, independent services. Each service can be developed, deployed, and scaled individually, enhancing the system's overall flexibility and maintainability.

Containerization tools like Docker facilitate consistent deployment across various environments by packaging applications and their dependencies into isolated containers.

Orchestration tools like Kubernetes can manage these containers, providing automated scaling, load balancing, and self-healing capabilities.

Monitoring and maintaining the deployed recommendation engine is vital for ensuring sustained performance. Implementing robust logging mechanisms helps track pipeline execution and detect errors promptly. Monitoring tools can provide real-time insights into model performance using metrics like throughput, latency, and error rates. Setting up alerts for anomalies ensures that any issues can be addressed before they impact user experience.

Summary for Creating A Recommendation System

- Install Python IDE on your computer.

- Use a code editor like Jupyter Notebook to edit your code. Use Docker as a containerization tool alongside Kubernetes as an orchestration tool to manage the containers.

- Use the Pandas library to import the dataset of users that you will use for your recommendations.

- Clean the data to remove duplicates—Store user data in NoSQL databases, using caching to store frequently accessed data for easy reference.

- Group users by identifying similar topics between them—use Collaborative filtering or Content-based filtering. Use Feature engineering combined with domain knowledge to create viable test data for your models. Train your models with the use of Matrix Factorization or Neural Networks algorithms.

- Monitor the recommendation system so that you can fine-tune it.

Designing a Real-Time Analytics Dashboard

Creating a real-time analytics dashboard is an essential skill for any data engineer or software developer working with large-scale data applications. you

Dashboards enable effective data visualization, presenting complex datasets in a manner that is both clear and actionable. Designing them requires an emphasis on clarity, accuracy, and efficiency.

Clarity ensures that the visualizations are easily understandable at a glance. For instance, using simple and well-labeled graphs can help users grasp key metrics without confusion.

Accuracy is vital to ensure the data presented is precise and reliable. Efficient use of visual space, minimalistic design, and selective highlighting of critical information contribute to a user-friendly experience.

Tools for Interactive Dashboards

Popular frameworks and libraries provide the backbone for building interactive dashboards. Tools like Plotly, Dash, and Streamlit offer robust features tailored to different needs.

Plotly is ideal for creating richly detailed and highly interactive visualizations. It supports a wide range of chart types, including 3D plots and heatmaps, making it versatile for various data storytelling requirements. Standalone Plotly is particularly suitable for embedding high-quality graphs within web pages or reports, offering extensive customization options and interactivity (Pavlovych, 2024).

Dash, developed by Plotly, stands out for its ease of use and seamless integration with Plotly's charting capabilities.

It abstracts much of the complexity associated with web development, enabling developers to create sophisticated dashboards using only Python code. This makes Dash a go-to choice for applications requiring real-time data updates, such as monitoring financial metrics or visualizing IoT data (Pavlovych, 2024).

Streamlit, another powerful tool, focuses on simplicity and rapid prototyping. It allows for quick deployment of interactive web applications with minimal code.

Streamlit's auto-reloading feature streamlines the development process by updating the application in real-time as the underlying code changes.

Its simple syntax and declarative approach make it accessible for creating functional products almost instantaneously, perfect for data science workflows and machine learning applications (Pavlovych, 2024).

Connecting and retrieving data from various sources is another critical aspect of building a real-time analytics dashboard. REST APIs and WebSockets are instrumental in this process.

- **REST APIs** facilitate communication between the dashboard and external data sources by allowing the dashboard to make HTTP requests to retrieve the necessary data. For example, an e-commerce dashboard might use a REST API to fetch sales data from an online store's database.

- **WebSockets**, on the other hand, provide a persistent connection that enables real-time data streaming. This is particularly useful for applications where live data updates are crucial, such as stock market dashboards or social media monitoring tools (Archer, 2023).

Ensuring the dashboard runs efficiently and scales effectively involves several strategies. Real-time data caching is one such strategy.

Caching improves performance by reducing the load on the server, thus minimizing response times.

Query optimization is another crucial tactic. Poorly written queries can lead to slow, non-performant dashboards. By following SQL best practices, such as filtering data before joining tables or indexing columns frequently used in WHERE clauses, you can significantly enhance query performance.

Another strategy is load balancing, which distributes incoming network traffic across multiple servers to ensure no single server becomes overloaded.

This helps maintain the reliability and availability of the dashboard, especially during peak usage times. Additionally, employing containerization tools like Docker can aid in consistent deployments and scaling.

Docker containers encapsulate the application and its dependencies, making it easier to manage and scale the dashboard across different environments (Archer, 2023.).

Visualizing complex datasets effectively requires a thoughtful approach to design principles. Clear labeling, appropriate axis scales, and the use of contrasting colors can significantly enhance readability.

The choice of visualization techniques should align with the type of data being presented. For instance, using a line graph to show trends over time is more effective than a pie chart. On the other hand, time-series data is best visualized using line charts or area charts, while categorical data may be better represented with bar charts or histograms.

Providing users with interactive elements, such as filters and drill-down capabilities, can further enhance the dashboard's utility.

These features allow users to customize their views and delve deeper into specific data points, leading to more meaningful insights. For example, a sales dashboard may include filters for different regions or product categories, enabling users to analyze data relevant to their specific interests or responsibilities.

When examining best practices employed in dashboards across various industries, we find that healthcare dashboards often utilize heatmaps to display patient data, while financial dashboards might employ candlestick charts to represent stock price movements. Consider these examples when called upon to display specific aspects so you can benefit from the proven effectiveness of different visualization techniques when addressing specific industry needs.

Selecting the right tech stack is crucial for building a functional and scalable dashboard. In addition to Plotly, Dash, and Streamlit, other tools like Highcharts and Retool offer diverse features for creating interactive visualizations. Highcharts, built on JavaScript and TypeScript, provide a wide range of flexible chart components suitable for visualizing important metrics.

Retool abstracts the complexities of frontend development into a series of drag-and-drop components, making it easy to build custom dashboards without extensive coding knowledge.

Backend databases and data platforms play a critical role in supporting real-time visualizations. Event streaming platforms and message queues, like Apache Kafka and Amazon Kinesis, capture and transmit data in real-time, ensuring the dashboard receives up-to-date information promptly.

In-memory databases and caching solutions, such as Redis or Memcached, further enhance performance by reducing latency and speeding up data retrieval.

Case Study: Optimizing Data Flow in E-Commerce

In this section, we explore a real-world case study in an e-commerce environment to highlight the optimization of data flow and application performance. E-commerce applications often face myriad challenges with data flow, significantly impacting user experience and operational efficiency.

Through this analysis, we aim to provide insights into common issues, effective optimization strategies, and the importance of continuous monitoring.

One of the prevalent data flow issues in e-commerce applications is data bottlenecks, which occur when the system's throughput capacity is overwhelmed by the volume of incoming data. This often results in slower page load times, delayed transaction processing, and, ultimately, a poor user experience.

Another issue is data redundancy, where duplicate data entries cause unnecessary load on databases, leading to inefficiencies and increased latency. Additionally, handling concurrent user requests during peak times can result in race conditions and deadlocks, further impairing performance.

System Performance Monitoring

To mitigate these issues, it is crucial to implement robust techniques for monitoring system performance. System performance monitoring involves tracking key metrics such as data flow rate, processing time, error rates, and resource utilization.

Tools like Grafana and Prometheus can be used to set up real-time dashboards that visualize these metrics, allowing developers to quickly identify and address bottlenecks.

By analyzing the data flow rate, one can determine whether the system's capacity needs scaling or whether specific processes are causing delays.

Improving data flow within an application requires strategic operations such as batching and asynchronous processing.

Batching operations consolidate multiple data transactions into a single operation, reducing the number of database hits and minimizing overhead. This approach is particularly useful in scenarios involving high-frequency transactions, such as adding items to a shopping cart or updating user preferences.

Asynchronous processing allows certain tasks to run in the background without blocking the main application thread. For example, sending confirmation emails asynchronously ensures that users do not experience delays during checkout.

Measuring the impact of these optimizations necessitates the use of Key Performance Indicators (KPIs) and post-deployment analysis.

KPIs such as Average Response Time, Throughput, and Error Rate are vital in quantifying the effectiveness of improvements.

Conducting A/B testing before and after implementing changes provides concrete evidence of their impact.

Post-deployment analysis involves continuously monitoring these KPIs to ensure that the optimizations yield sustained benefits over time. Tools such as New Relic and DataDog are instrumental in providing deep insights into application performance and helping teams make informed decisions.

Latency Improvement Case Study

A compelling case study that illustrates these principles involved an e-commerce company facing severe latency issues during high-traffic events like Black Friday. Initially, the system struggled with processing high volumes of transactions, resulting in:

- slow response times

- lost sales opportunities

A thorough analysis revealed that inefficient data flow was the primary culprit. The team addressed this by implementing:

- batching for order processing

- asynchronous inventory updates

These changes significantly improved throughput, reducing the average response time by 40%.

Additionally, the company adopted a comprehensive monitoring strategy using tools that provided real-time insights into system performance. This enabled them to proactively identify potential bottlenecks before they escalated into critical issues.

They also established KPIs tailored to their operational goals, ensuring that each optimization had measurable outcomes. The success of these strategies was evident through a substantial increase in customer satisfaction and a notable boost in sales.

From this case study, several critical lessons emerge.

1. First, continuous monitoring is essential for maintaining optimal performance. It allows teams to detect and resolve issues promptly, ensuring that the application runs smoothly even under heavy loads.

2. Second, cross-team collaboration plays a pivotal role in successful optimization projects. Involving diverse expertise from developers, database administrators, and network specialists fosters a holistic approach to problem-solving.

3. Finally, fostering a culture of experimentation encourages innovation and iterative improvement.

By conducting regular tests and analyses, teams can explore new optimization techniques and stay ahead of evolving challenges.

Lessons Learned

In this chapter, we explored practical projects and real-world examples to understand advanced concepts in designing data-intensive applications using Python. We delved into building a scalable recommendation system by examining collaborative and content-based filtering techniques, hybrid methods, and the importance of effective data storage solutions like SQL and NoSQL databases.

Additionally, we discussed the role of caching mechanisms and the necessity of training and evaluating machine learning models for high-quality recommendations. Effective deployment strategies and monitoring practices were also highlighted to ensure the longevity and efficiency of recommendation engines.

Furthermore, we covered the essential skills needed to create a real-time analytics dashboard. This included selecting appropriate data visualization tools such as Plotly, Dash, and Streamlit, as well as integrating data sources through REST APIs and WebSockets. Strategies for improving performance and scalability, including query optimization, load balancing, and the use of containerization tools, were also examined.

Clear design principles and interactive features were emphasized to enhance user experience. By providing these insights and methodologies, the chapter equipped you with the knowledge to tackle complex data-intensive tasks effectively.

Now that you know how to implement a recommendation dashboard, you can combine this with the knowledge you gained from the other chapters and get ready to apply your knowledge in the real world.

One of the first steps toward this knowledge application is to work in an appropriate role within the IT engineering sector. The next chapter will prepare you for this by providing you with guidance on how to approach data system design interview.

CHAPTER 10

Preparing for Data System Design Interviews

Preparing for data system design interviews requires a comprehensive approach that demonstrates an understanding of both theoretical concepts and their practical applications.

As the realm of data engineering continues to evolve, candidates must be adept at:

- navigating through complex systems.

- addressing scalability issues.

- ensuring data consistency.

- mitigating latency concerns.

- fortifying security measures.

The sample interview questions and answers provided below will give you an understanding of what kind of questions to expect from your interview, the type of responses that you can provide, and the expected level of knowledge that helps you adequately address these and similar questions.

Example Interview Questions and Answers

Here are some questions and their answers for a Python Data Systems Design interview:

Question 1:

What are the key principles to consider when designing a data system?

Answer: Key principles include:

- scalability (ability to handle growth)

- reliability (ensuring consistent operation)

- maintainability (ease of updates)

- performance (efficiency in data processing)

- security (protecting data access and integrity)

Additionally, data models should be designed according to the specific use cases, such as OLAP (Online Analytical Processing) or OLTP (Online Transaction Processing).

Question 2:

How would you design a data pipeline for real-time data processing?

Answer: A real-time data pipeline can be designed using message brokers (e.g., Apache Kafka) to collect data, followed by stream processing frameworks (e.g., Apache Spark or Flink) for real-time transformations. Finally, the processed data can be stored in a data store optimized for read/write operations (e.g., a NoSQL database like MongoDB or a data warehouse like Google BigQuery). Ensuring minimal latency and high throughput should be key considerations.

Latency remains a significant concern in data-intensive applications, directly impacting system performance and user experience. High latency can lead to delayed responses, frustrating end-users and diminishing the system's overall effectiveness.

To mitigate latency issues, various techniques can be deployed. Caching frequently accessed data is a straightforward solution that reduces the need to repeatedly query the primary database, significantly speeding up response times.

Asynchronous processing separates the task execution from the user's request, allowing the system to continue processing information in the background without making users wait.

Additionally, message queuing systems like RabbitMQ or Apache Kafka help manage the flow of data between services, enabling efficient communication and processing across different components without increasing latency. These methods collectively contribute to smoother, faster interactions within the system, enhancing user satisfaction.

Data pipelines are often discussed in interviews because they are central to modern data systems. One crucial decision is selecting the appropriate streaming tools. Apache Kafka, for instance, is commonly recommended due to its high throughput, scalability, and fault tolerance.

Candidates should be able to explain why they would choose Kafka or another tool based on specific requirements such as message delivery guarantees and latency considerations.

Additionally, discuss the nuances of data processing options—like stream processing tools (e.g., Apache Flink) versus batch processing—and storage options, emphasizing the criteria for choosing between data lakes and data warehouses.

Data lakes, with their ability to store raw, unprocessed data, are suitable for exploratory analysis, whereas data warehouses are optimized for structured querying and reporting.

Question 3:
How do you handle schema evolution in a data system?

Answer: Schema evolution can be managed by using a versioning system for the data schema or by employing flexible schema formats like Avro or Parquet.

When changing the schema, backward compatibility should be maintained, allowing older data to be read with the new schema without issue. Implementing strategies such as adding new fields with default values or using nullable fields can help accommodate changes.

Demonstrating an understanding of data modeling schemas can be beneficial. You might cover the star schema, which organizes data into fact tables linked to dimension tables, and the snowflake schema, which normalizes dimension tables into multiple related tables. Understanding these schemas highlights your capability to design efficient data structures suited to various analytical queries.

Question 4:

What strategies can be used for data partitioning in a large-scale database?

Answer: Data partitioning strategies include horizontal partitioning (sharding) to split tables into smaller chunks based on key ranges or user IDs, vertical partitioning to separate columns into different tables based on access patterns, and time-based partitioning for time-series data. Choosing a proper partitioning key and monitoring access patterns are critical for optimizing performance and query efficiency.

When discussing large-scale databases, candidates must show familiarity with sharding, replication, and load balancing techniques. Sharding divides a database into smaller, more manageable pieces called shards, which can be distributed across multiple servers to improve performance and scalability.

Replication involves copying data across multiple servers to increase availability and reliability. Load balancing ensures that no single server bears too much load by distributing traffic evenly.

Managing the challenges posed by increased data volume in applications is fundamental in the realm of data engineering. As applications grow, they often encounter limitations that threaten their capability to handle massive datasets effectively.

To address this, one must consider both horizontal and vertical scaling strategies. Vertical scaling involves upgrading a single machine's capacity by adding more resources, such as CPU or RAM, which can provide a quick fix but has its limits.

Alternatively, horizontal scaling spreads the workload across multiple servers, offering a more sustainable approach to managing extensive data volumes.

Central to these strategies is the practice of data partitioning, which segments large datasets into smaller, more manageable chunks distributed across several nodes.

This approach not only enhances data processing efficiency but also ensures that no single node bears the brunt of the workload, thus promoting system stability and scalability (*Key Challenges and Solutions for Database Scalability*, 2024).

Another critical aspect of managing data systems that you will need to keep in mind is that of addressing data consistency within distributed environments. Inconsistencies can arise due to the distributed nature of modern systems, leading to challenges in maintaining uniform data states across different nodes.

Trade-offs between eventual consistency and strong consistency models must be carefully considered. Eventual consistency allows for temporary discrepancies between nodes, with the expectation that all nodes will eventually align. This model supports high availability but at the cost of temporary inconsistencies.

On the other hand, strong consistency ensures that every read receives the most recent write, providing reliable and predictable data at the expense of performance and availability.

Using distributed databases like Apache Cassandra or Google Spanner helps maintain data integrity by leveraging replication and coordination mechanisms to synchronize data across nodes, ensuring consistent states across the entire system (*What Is Data Partitioning? And How It Leads to Efficient Data Processing | Airbyte*, n.d.).

Question 5:
Discuss the trade-offs between SQL and NoSQL databases in data systems design.

Answer: SQL databases provide ACID (Atomicity, Consistency, Isolation, Durability) properties, making them suitable for applications requiring complex queries and transactions. They work well with structured data. However, they may face challenges in scalability.

On the other hand, NoSQL databases offer flexibility in data models (e.g., document, key-value, column-family) and are easier to scale horizontally. They sacrifice some consistency for availability, making them better suited for large-scale, distributed systems where speed is a priority.

Choosing between them depends on the specific requirements of the application, including data structure, query needs, and scalability goals.

Interviewees should know how to address the choice between SQL and NoSQL databases. SQL databases, known for their structured query language and ACID (Atomicity, Consistency, Isolation, Durability) properties, are ideal for transactions requiring strong consistency. In contrast, NoSQL databases offer flexibility and scalability, making them suitable for applications dealing with large volumes of unstructured data.

Common Industry Problems and Solutions

Preparing for data system design interviews requires a thorough understanding of common interview questions and structured answers like the ones in the examples above. You can increase your level of preparation by exploring key topics such as designing data pipelines, scaling databases, ensuring data quality, and handling data system outages. By being prepared for questions pertaining to these topics, you will be better equipped to face these discussions confidently.

Security Considerations

Security vulnerabilities in data-intensive applications are another paramount concern, especially given the sensitive nature of the data being processed. Ensuring robust security measures is crucial to protect both data at rest and data in transit.

Encryption plays a vital role here; encrypting data ensures that even if it is intercepted during transmission or accessed unlawfully, it remains unreadable without the decryption key.

Identifying potential attack vectors, such as SQL injection or phishing, enables developers to implement targeted safeguards, further securing the application. Compliance with regulations like GDPR is essential, as these laws mandate strict protocols for data protection and user privacy.

Organizations must ensure they adhere to these guidelines to avoid hefty penalties and maintain user trust. Implementing these best practices fortifies the application's defense against unauthorized access and data breaches.

Addressing Questions About Data Quality

Ensuring data quality in pipelines is another critical topic. Prospective data engineers should demonstrate knowledge of validation, cleansing, and profiling methods.

Validation checks that data meets specific criteria before processing. Cleansing involves correcting errors and inconsistencies in the data, while profiling assesses the data's overall quality and completeness.

Automated data quality tools, such as Talend or Informatica, can streamline these processes, reducing manual effort and enhancing accuracy. Implementing a culture of data stewardship within an organization further bolsters data quality by emphasizing accountability and best practices throughout the data lifecycle.

How to Handle A Systems Outage

Addressing data system outages requires a methodical approach. When a system outage occurs, the first step is diagnosing the issue.

This typically involves checking logs, monitoring system metrics, and identifying any recent changes that could have triggered the problem.

Collaboration during incident response is vital; teams must communicate effectively to resolve the issue promptly.

Once the immediate issue is addressed, it's essential to implement process enhancements based on lessons learned. This might include updating documentation, refining monitoring systems, and conducting post-mortem analyses to prevent similar incidents in the future.

Addressing Data Migration Questions

Interviews may include questions about your experience and knowledge in these areas. For example, you might be asked how you would validate a data migration from one database to another.

A robust answer would cover various validation types, ranging from simple comparisons to comprehensive post-migration checks, ensuring no data is lost or corrupted during the transfer.

You could also be asked about your experience with ETL (Extract, Transform, Load) processes and tools. Detailing your familiarity with tools like Apache NiFi, Talend, or Microsoft SSIS and explaining your preference based on the project requirements would demonstrate your practical knowledge.

Discussing Hadoop

Questions regarding Hadoop and its components are also common. You should be prepared to discuss Hadoop's relationship with big data and describe its core components:

- HDFS (Hadoop Distributed File System)

- MapReduce

- Hadoop Common

- YARN (Yet Another Resource Negotiator)

Each component plays a crucial role in processing and managing large datasets efficiently. For instance, HDFS provides high-throughput access to application data, while MapReduce performs data processing on vast amounts of data in parallel.

Principles of Big Data

Finally, discussing big data's four Vs volume, velocity, variety, and veracity can effectively illustrate your grasp of significant data engineering principles.

Volume refers to the sheer amount of data, while velocity deals with the speed at which data is generated and processed.

Variety covers the different types of data, such as structured and unstructured data, and veracity addresses data quality and accuracy.

Proficiently managing these aspects is crucial for deriving value from big data and supporting business decisions.

Tips for Articulating Your Approach

Clear Communication During System Design Interviews

Preparing for data system design interviews is not just about understanding the technical concepts; it's also about effectively communicating your knowledge.

One key to succeeding in these interviews is to articulate your answers clearly and succinctly. This ability leaves a positive impression on the interviewers and demonstrates not only your technical skills but also your communication prowess.

During the interview, it's crucial to take moments to pause and reflect. This practice serves several purposes.

First, brief pauses allow you to organize your thoughts before responding, ensuring that your answers are well-structured and coherent. They also give you time to manage any anxiety and avoid rushing through your responses.

Clear articulation of your reasoning is vital; it not only demonstrates confidence but also allows the interviewer to follow your thought process and understand your decision-making criteria.

In addition, sharing techniques for managing interview anxiety can be invaluable. Practicing deep breathing exercises, maintaining a positive mindset, and visualizing a successful interview can all help you stay calm and focused.

Remember that it's perfectly acceptable to take a moment to think before answering a question. This approach shows mindfulness and a deliberate thought process, which are critical attributes for roles involving system design.

Structure Your Responses

Establishing a clear structure for your responses can significantly enhance your ability to convey your ideas logically and concisely.

Frameworks like STAR (Situation, Task, Action, Result) provide an excellent foundation. Start by outlining the situation or context of the problem you are addressing.

Then, define the specific task or challenge you faced. Next, detail the actions you took to tackle the issue, and finally, describe the results of your efforts.

This methodical approach helps interviewers follow your thought process and showcases your problem-solving skills clearly.

Provide Context For Your Responses

It's equally important to establish a context before diving into technical details.

By setting the stage, you help the interviewer understand why certain decisions were made and how they align with the overall goal.

This context can include the scope of the project, the constraints you had to work within, and any unique challenges you encountered.

Establishing this background information ensures that your subsequent technical explanations are more meaningful and easier to grasp.

Expand Your Answers With Examples and Anecdotes

Using relevant examples from past experiences can further enhance your responses. Describing specific projects you've worked on not only illustrates your expertise but also shows how you apply your knowledge practically.

When discussing these examples, relate them to the job description or the company's context. Highlight how your experience aligns with the requirements of the role you're interviewing for.

This alignment reassures the interviewer that you are a good fit for the position and familiar with the type of work you'll be doing.

Similarly, it's beneficial to prepare a mental library of anecdotes that you can use during interviews. These stories should illustrate key skills or experiences relevant to the job.

By having these examples ready, you can quickly draw upon them to answer various questions, demonstrating your versatility and depth of experience.

Solicit feedback from peers or mentors to refine your interview skills further. Role-playing interviews with colleagues enables you to simulate the interview environment and receive constructive criticism.

This practice allows you to identify areas for improvement and build confidence through repetition. Additionally, using mock interview platforms can provide a realistic practice environment where you can hone your skills and get accustomed to the types of questions that may be asked.

Continuous learning and refinement of your answers based on feedback and experiences play a crucial role in improving your performance in interviews.

After each practice session, take time to reflect on what went well and what could be improved.

Adjust your responses accordingly and practice until you feel confident and prepared. The more you practice, the more natural and polished your answers will become, increasing your chances of making a positive impression during the actual interview.

Summary and Reflections

This chapter has explored some typical interview questions and provided guidance on how to answer them. It has further explored the essential strategies and tools necessary for excelling in system design interviews, particularly those geared toward data engineering roles.

It has covered various critical aspects, including managing increased data volumes through vertical and horizontal scaling, ensuring data consistency in distributed environments, and mitigating latency issues with techniques such as caching and asynchronous processing.

The chapter also discussed the importance of robust security measures to protect sensitive data and adhere to regulations, ultimately ensuring the stability and security of data-intensive applications.

By understanding and applying these concepts, you will be better equipped to tackle common challenges faced in designing and managing large-scale data systems.

This knowledge will not only enhance your technical capabilities but also prepare you to articulate your approach clearly during interviews.

The ability to communicate complex ideas in a structured and concise manner is crucial for success in system design interviews. As you continue to refine your skills and gain practical experience, you will find yourself more confident and prepared to excel in your data engineering careers.

Conclusion

During this journey, you've learned to distinguish between data-intensive and CPU-intensive systems. You have grasped essential data engineering concepts and appreciated how Python can facilitate the construction of robust, scalable applications. We've delved into the nitty-gritty of designing and optimizing data-intensive applications, equipping you with a solid foundation upon which to build.

As we revisit these foundational principles, recognize that they form the backbone of everything you've learned. Understanding the distinction between data-intensive and CPU-intensive systems allows you to make informed decisions about resource allocation and optimization. This understanding is not just theoretical—it directly impacts your ability to design efficient and effective data systems in real-world scenarios.

Modern tools such as Apache Kafka and Kubernetes have been highlighted in your exploration of data engineering. Your exposure to Apache Kafka for data streaming and Kubernetes for managing containerized applications equips you to navigate emerging technologies in the ever-evolving data engineering landscape.

These tools are at the forefront of current industry practices, and mastering them will give you a competitive edge. They enable you to handle large-scale data processing and manage complex systems with ease, making your work more efficient and scalable.

One of the core themes we've stressed throughout the book is the value of hands-on practice. Theory alone cannot make you proficient in building data systems; it's the practical application that truly cements your knowledge.

By engaging with projects that teach practical skills, such as building a data pipeline and a scalable recommendation system, you have translated complex concepts into actionable skills, positioning and building a scalable recommendation system, you as a capable builder of data systems.

These projects were designed to mimic real-world challenges, giving you a taste of what to expect in professional settings. The experience you've gained through these exercises is invaluable; it's where theory meets reality and where true learning happens.

Looking ahead, preparing for system design interviews is a significant step for those of you aiming to enter or advance in the tech industry. The knowledge you've gained from this book can be directly applied to real-world industry challenges and career advancement.

The ability to clearly explain your thought process and solutions is often as important as the technical solution itself.

Your path is filled with opportunities to grow and excel. Hands-on practice implementing the snippets of code provided has transformed theoretical knowledge into practical skills. Embracing modern tools like Apache Kafka and Kubernetes places you at the cutting edge of the field, ready to take on complex tasks with efficiency and precision.

Armed with insights into industry problems and refined articulation of your approach, you're now better positioned to impress potential employers in data system design interviews. Preparing for system design interviews with the insights you've gained will improve your chances of securing your desired role in the industry. And finally, maintaining a mindset of lifelong learning will ensure you continue to grow professionally and stay relevant in an ever-changing landscape.

As you come to the end of this book, it's important to recognize that this is just the beginning of your learning process. The field of data engineering is vast and constantly evolving, and continued learning is crucial to staying ahead.

Keeping abreast of new developments in data engineering will help you address the challenges that you might face in this evolving world of data manipulation. Without continued learning, you might find yourself facing new tools that can be difficult to master.

There is a wealth of resources available, from academic papers and industry blogs to community forums and open-source projects. These resources can provide you with new insights, help you solve problems, and keep you up-to-date with the latest developments.

Becoming part of a community can significantly boost your learning experience. Interacting with peers and experts, sharing knowledge, and collaborating on projects can provide you with different perspectives and innovative approaches to problem-solving.

Engaging with online forums, participating in workshops, and pursuing advanced tutorials will only enhance your expertise and keep you at the forefront of the field. Therefore, it is important that you seek out and join online and in-person communities with those involved in the field of data. These interactions can also lead to networking opportunities, which can be beneficial for career growth. Sites you can start with include LinkedIn, Stack Overflow, and GitHub.

We hope this book has been a valuable resource in your journey toward becoming a proficient data engineer. Remember, the world of data engineering is boundless, and your potential within it is limitless. Keep exploring, keep learning, and most importantly, keep building. Start with a data project today to help you implement everything you have learned. The future is yours to shape, one data system at a time.

Installation Steps

This section provides installation steps when deploying a Kubernetes application. It provides further detail to the instructions in Chapter 3.

Installing Apache Kafka

To install Apache Kafka, follow these detailed steps:

Prerequisites:

Java Installation: Make sure you have Java installed on your system. Kafka requires Java 8 or higher.

To check if Java is already installed, run:

```
java -version
```

If not installed, download and install the latest version of Java from Oracle's Java downloads (https://www.oracle.com/java/technologies/javase-jdk11-downloads.html) or via your package manager.

Download Kafka:

Visit the Apache Kafka downloads page (https://kafka.apache.org/downloads) and download the latest release.

Alternatively, you can use wget to download it directly to your terminal:

```
wget    https://downloads.apache.org/kafka/x.y.z/kafka_2.13-
x.y.z.tgz
```

Replace x.y.z with the current version number.

Extract the Downloaded Archive:

Run the following command to extract the contents:

```
tar -xzf kafka_2.13-x.y.z.tgz
```

Navigate into the extracted Kafka directory:

```
cd kafka_2.13-x.y.z
```

Installation Process:

Start Zookeeper:

Kafka uses Zookeeper for managing distributed brokers. You can start Zookeeper using the command:

```
bin/zookeeper-server-start.sh config/zookeeper.properties
```

This command runs Zookeeper in the foreground. You can open a new terminal window for the next steps.

Start Kafka Server:

In the new terminal window, start the Kafka server by running:

```
bin/kafka-server-start.sh config/server.properties
```

This will also run in the foreground.

Create a Topic:

To create a topic named test, use the following command in a new terminal:

```
bin/kafka-topics.sh --create --topic test --bootstrap-server
localhost:9092 --partitions 1 --replication-factor 1
```

List Topics:

You can verify the topic creation by listing all topics:

```
bin/kafka-topics.sh --list --bootstrap-server localhost:9092
```

Start a Producer:

To send messages to the topic, start a producer:

```
bin/kafka-console-producer.sh --topic test --bootstrap-server
localhost:9092
```

Type messages and press Enter to send them.

Start a Consumer:

In another terminal window, start a consumer to read the messages:

```
bin/kafka-console-consumer.sh --topic test --from-beginning -
-bootstrap-server localhost:9092
```

Verification:

You should see the messages sent from the producer displayed in the consumer terminal.

Stopping the Services:

- To stop the consumer and producer, use Ctrl + C.

- To stop the Kafka server and Zookeeper, use the same command in their respective terminal windows.

Kafka Installation Complete

By this point you will have successfully installed Apache Kafka, created a topic, and sent and received messages. For further configuration and operational guidance, refer to the Apache Kafka documentation(kafka.apache.org/documentation).

Step-by-Step Instructions for Creating a Docker Image of Your Python Application

Install Docker:

Ensure that Docker is installed on your machine. You can download it from the Docker website (https://www.docker.com/get-started).

Create Your Python Application:

Write your Python application code in a directory. For example, create a folder named my_python_app and add a file app.py.

Add Requirements File:

If your application requires external packages, create a requirements.txt file in the same directory and list the packages there.

Create a Dockerfile:

```
# Use the official Python image from Docker Hub
FROM python:3.8-slim

# Set the working directory inside the container
WORKDIR /app

# Copy the requirements.txt file to the container
COPY requirements.txt .
```

```
# Install the dependencies
RUN pip install --no-cache-dir -r requirements.txt

# Copy the rest of the application code to the container
COPY . .

# Specify the command to run the application
CMD ["python", "app.py"]
```

In the my_python_app directory, create a file named Dockerfile (without any extension) and add the following content:

Build the Docker Image:

```
docker build -t my_python_app .
```

Open a terminal or command prompt, navigate to the my_python_app directory, and run the following command to build the Docker image:

Run the Docker Container:

```
docker run my_python_app
```

Once the image is built, you can run the application using the following command:

Verify the Application:

Check the output in the terminal to ensure that your Python application is running as expected.

Optional - Manage the Image:

You can view all Docker images on your machine with:

```
docker images
```

To remove the image, use:

```
docker rmi my_python_app
```

Docker Image Creation Complete

By this point, you will have successfully created and run a Docker image for your Python application and can continue deploying your Kubernetes application.

Kubernetes Installation

Here are the step-by-step instructions for installing Kubernetes using kubeadm on a Linux system:

Step 1: Prepare Your System

Update your package list:

```
sudo apt-get update
```

Install required packages:

```
sudo apt-get install -y apt-transport-https ca-certificates
curl
```

Add Docker's official GPG key:

```
curl -fsSL https://download.docker.com/linux/ubuntu/gpg |
sudo apt-key add -
```

Set up the stable repository:

```
echo "deb [arch=amd64]
https://download.docker.com/linux/ubuntu $(lsb_release -cs)
stable" | sudo tee /etc/apt/sources.list.d/docker.list
```

Update your package list again:

```
sudo apt-get update
```

Install Docker:

```
sudo apt-get install -y docker-ce
```

Step 2: Install Kubernetes Components

Add the Kubernetes GPG key:

```
curl -s https://packages.cloud.google.com/apt/doc/apt-key.gpg
| sudo apt-key add -
```

Add the Kubernetes repository:

```
echo "deb https://apt.kubernetes.io/ kubernetes-xenial main" |
sudo tee /etc/apt/sources.list.d/kubernetes.list
```

Update your package list again:

```
sudo apt-get update
```

Install kubelet, kubeadm, and kubectl:

```
sudo apt-get install -y kubelet kubeadm kubectl
```

Mark them to hold back updates:

```
sudo apt-mark hold kubelet kubeadm kubectl
```

Step 3: Initialize Your Kubernetes Cluster

Initialize the cluster:

```
sudo kubeadm init
```

Set up the local kubeconfig file for the regular user:

```
mkdir -p $HOME/.kube
sudo cp -i /etc/kubernetes/admin.conf $HOME/.kube/config
sudo chown $(id -u):$(id -g) $HOME/.kube/config
```

Step 4: Set Up a Network Plugin

Install a network plugin (e.g., Weave Net):

```
kubectl apply -f https://cloud.weave.works/k8s/net?k8s-
version=$(kubectl version --short | awk -Fv '/Server
Version/{print $2}')
```

Step 5: Join Worker Nodes

Run the join command provided by kubeadm on each worker node: (Use the command that was output after initializing the cluster)

Step 6: Verify the Cluster

Check the status of nodes:

```
kubectl get nodes
```

Installation Complete

By now you will have a running Kubernetes cluster.

Glossary

- **API:** A software whose acronym stands for Application Programming Interface. It defines the method that can be used by others to access an application or specific service on a server.

- **Cassandra:** A noSQL distributed database developed by Apache.

- **CPU-Intensive Systems:** Systems that focus on computational performance.

- **CPU Utilization:** A measure of the CPU cycles that are used to perform any given task.

- **Data-Intensive Applications:** Applications that store, retrieve, and process data.

- **DataFrame:** A two-dimensional layout of data that is structured similarly to a relational database or a spreadsheet.

- **Distributed Database:** A database that is stored across multiple servers.

- **Domain Knowledge:** Having expertise in a particular industry.

- **Elasticsearch Stack (ELK):** A platform that analyzes, searches, visualizes, and formats data.

- **ETL:** Extract, Transform, and Load method for data transfer and use.

- **Grafana:** An open-source analytics tool that provides feedback using prompts and a visual interface.

- **gPRC:** A Remote Procedures Call framework created by Google. It is open-source and used to enable communication between different applications.

- **H-Base:** A non-relational distributed database built by Apache to run on the Hadoop Distributed File System(HDFS).

- **High-Performance Computing Cluster:** A collection of servers in which each server is referred to as a node. The nodes perform the parallel processing of tasks related to large amounts of data.

- **JMeter:** A Java application developed by Apache. It is used to simulate network loads when testing the capacity of a system.

- **Memory Usage:** A measure of server efficiency due to the amount of Random Access Memory (RAM) that different processes use.

- **Microservices Architecture:** An approach that breaks down an application into smaller units that focus on specific micro-activities.

- **Network Throughput:** The package delivery capacity of a network. It is influenced by bandwidth, latency, and network speed.

- **Parallel Processing:** A method that breaks tasks down into separate components. This enables the processing of the tasks to be carried out across multiple central processing units(CPUs).

- **Prometheus:** A solution that can be installed within Kubernetes or as a standalone server. It can be used to monitor infrastructure and systems applications. The server provides alerts and notifications via third-party tools when pre-defined metrics are reached.

- **PEP 8 Coding Conventions:** Guidelines for coding in Python. This includes naming conventions for variables, classes, and functions.

- **REST:** Within API's REST is Representational State Transfer. Therefore RESTful API's do not maintain a state. Instead they assume the state that is passed on to them via the requesting service.

- **SSL Offloading:** A mechanism through which the secure server layer encryption of an incoming data package is processed and removed before it is passed on to the server. This leaves more server resources for processing and responding to the query.

- **VisualVM:** A tool for viewing and troubleshooting Java applications while they are running.

References

Adepoju, F. (2021, April 26). *An Introduction to asynchronous processing and message queues*. Hookdeck. https://medium.com/hookdeck/an-introduction-to-asynchronous-processing-and-message-queues-218af596bf1b

Badshah, A. (2024, March 25). *Introduction to machine learning*. Medium. https://afzalbadshah.medium.com/introduction-to-machine-learning-f527d27156f8

AlphaCodes. (2021, October 7). *System design 101-everything to know about distributed systems....* DEV Community. https://dev.to/mukulalpha/system-design-101-everything-to-know-about-distributed-systems-2hd6

AnalytixLabs. (2024, June 26). *How to Use Python for data engineering*. Medium. https://medium.com/@byanalytixlabs/how-to-use-python-for-data-engineering-011528460024

Archer, C. (2023, August 8). *Real-time data visualization: how to build faster dashboards*. Tinybird. https://www.tinybird.co/blog-posts/real-time-data-visualization

August, G. (2024, January 9). *Enhancing data flows: effective monitoring and performance optimization in data engineering pipelines*. Medium. https://medium.com/@gadnwachukwu2/enhancing-data-flows-effective-monitoring-and-performance-optimization-in-data-engineering-d96feec6abd3

binhnguyennus. (2017). *The patterns of scalable, reliable, and performant large-scale systems*. GitHub. https://github.com/binhnguyennus/awesome-scalability

Barba, C. (Alumni. (2022, November 3). *PPC analysis case study: maximizing profit without maximizing ROAS*. Inflow. https://www.goinflow.com/blog/ecommerce-data-analysis-case-study/

Big O notation in data structure: an introduction. (2022, September 1). Simplilearn.com. https://www.simplilearn.com/big-o-notation-in-data-structure-article

Caching guidance - Azure architecture center. (n.d.). Learn.microsoft.com. https://learn.microsoft.com/en-us/azure/architecture/best-practices/caching

Dashboard anything. Observe everything. (n.d.) Grafana Labs. https://grafana.com/grafana/

Data engineering 101: lifecycle, best practices, and emerging trends. (2018). Redpanda.com. https://www.redpanda.com/guides/fundamentals-of-data-engineering

Data manipulation in Python using Pandas. (2020, May 1). GeeksforGeeks. https://www.geeksforgeeks.org/data-manipulattion-in-python-using-pandas/

Data visualization with Python Seaborn. (2020, December 2). GeeksforGeeks. https://www.geeksforgeeks.org/data-visualization-with-python-seaborn/

Difference between Jupyter and Pycharm. (2020, July 15). GeeksforGeeks. https://www.geeksforgeeks.org/difference-between-jupyter-and-pycharm/

Dixit, D. (2023, April 11). *PEP 8 tutorial: code standards in Python.* DataCamp. https://www.datacamp.com/tutorial/pep8-tutorial-python-code

Dom, N. (2022, November 8). *The data engineering lifecycle.* Medium. https://medium.com/@dom.n/the-data-engineering-lifecycle-5c67bf6fb540

14 data engineer interview questions and how to answer them. (2024). Coursera. https://www.coursera.org/articles/data-engineer-interview-questions

Gillis, A. (n.d.). *What is REST API (restful API)?* SearchAppArchitecture. https://www.techtarget.com/searchapparchitecture/definition/RESTful-API

Graph theory in data science: applications and algorithms. (2024, February 15). Dataheadhunters.com. https://dataheadhunters.com/academy/graph-theory-in-data-science-applications-and-algorithms/

High-performance computing. (n.d). Nvidia. https://www.nvidia.com/en-us/glossary/high-performance-computing/

How to ace interviews with the STAR method [9+ examples]. (n.d.). Novorésumé. https://novoresume.com/career-blog/interview-star-method

How to efficiently build scalable machine learning pipelines-explained in simple terms with implementation details. (2024). Substack.com; Ignito. https://naina0405.substack.com/p/how-to-efficiently-build-scalable-ce0

How to install numpy and matplotlib in the right Python version?. (2024). Stack Overflow. https://stackoverflow.com/questions/35766037/how-to-install-numpy-and-matplotlib-in-the-right-python-version

How to use Apache Kafka for real-time data streaming? (2024, March 21). ProjectPro. https://www.projectpro.io/article/kafka-for-real-time-streaming/916

Installing scikit-learn. (n.d.). Scikit-Learn. https://scikit-learn.org/stable/install.html

Introduction to Conda for (data) scientists. (2020). Github.io; The Carpentries Incubator - Introduction to Conda for (Data) Scientists. https://carpentries-incubator.github.io/introduction-to-conda-for-data-scientists/aio/index.html

Israel. (2023, September 3). *Event-driven architecture and message queues.* Medium. https://oluwadaprof.medium.com/event-driven-%EF%B8%8F-architecture-and-message-queues-bdd0383bf989

Kafka Streams vs. Apache Flink: A detailed comparison for real-time stream processing. (2024, May 8). RisingWave: Open-Source Streaming SQL Platform. https://risingwave.com/blog/kafka-streams-vs-apache-flink-a-detailed-comparison-for-real-time-stream-processing/

Key challenges and solutions for database scalability. (2024, June 29). RisingWave: Open-Source Streaming SQL Platform. https://risingwave.com/blog/key-challenges-and-solutions-for-database-scalability/

Kilonzi, F. (2022, November 10). *Graph theory using Python - introduction and implementation*. ActiveState. https://www.activestate.com/blog/graph-theory-using-python-introduction-and-implementation/

Kleppmann, M. (2017). *Designing data-intensive applications [Book]*. Www.oreilly.com. https://www.oreilly.com/library/view/designing-data-intensive-applications/9781491903063/ch01.html

Mullapudi, M. (2024, June 18). *Mastering distributed systems: essential design patterns for scalability and resilience*. Medium. https://tutorialq.medium.com/mastering-distributed-systems-essential-design-patterns-for-scalability-and-resilience-36a806360d3e

Meet the search platform that helps you search, solve, and succeed. (n.d.). Elastic Stack. https://www.elastic.co/elastic-stack

Mudadla, S. (2024, January 24). *What are the key components of a data pipeline, and how do they contribute to the efficient flow of data in an organization's data infrastructure?*. Medium. https://medium.com/@sujathamudadla1213/what-are-the-key-components-of-a-data-pipeline-and-how-do-they-contribute-to-the-efficient-flow-of-0fc5fc1d0bfd

Olawale, A. (2024, August 8). *Understanding data structures and algorithms*. Medium; Medium. https://medium.com/@Adekola_Olawale/understanding-data-structures-and-algorithms-758f86a7196d

Onyeanuna, P. (2024, June 26). *How does real-time data streaming work in Kafka?*. EverythingDevOps; EverythingDevOps. https://everythingdevops.dev/how-does-real-time-data-streaming-work-in-kafka/

Pavlovych, A. (2024, July 25). *What Is the best Python dashboard framework?*. PLANEKS. https://www.planeks.net/python-dashboard-development-framework/

Performance optimization in software architecture. (2024, July 9). [X]Cube LABS. https://www.xcubelabs.com/blog/performance-optimization-in-software-architecture/

Pierre, S. (2023, February 16). *A comprehensive guide to Python data visualization with Matplotlib and Seaborn*. Built In. https://builtin.com/data-science/data-visualization-tutorial

Prakash, A. (2023, July 11). *What Is data partitioning: types techniques and examples*. Airbyte.com. https://airbyte.com/data-engineering-resources/what-is-data-partitioning

Production-grade container orchestration. (2019). Kubernetes.io. https://kubernetes.io/

Power of etl automation tools and Python. (2023, July 14). ActiveBatch. https://www.advsyscon.com/blog/etl-automation-with-python/

Pucariello, G. (2024, May 6). *Apache Flink versus Apache Kafka—a deep dive into real-time processing powerhouses*. Data Reply IT | DataTech. https://medium.com/data-reply-it-datatech/apache-flink-versus-apache-kafka-a-deep-dive-into-real-time-processing-powerhouses-0d8ba9c9657e

Pykes, K. (2023, April 14). *Python machine learning: Scikit-learn tutorial*. Www.datacamp.com. https://www.datacamp.com/tutorial/machine-learning-python

Raj, M. (2024, January 27) *Optimizing SQL queries for peak performance*. Medium. https://medium.com/@maddyraj/optimizing-sql-queries-for-peak-performance-13cc9b6704f3

REST API architectural constraints. (2018, December 9). GeeksforGeeks. https://www.geeksforgeeks.org/rest-api-architectural-constraints/

Ritesh. (2024, July 4). *Monitoring with Prometheus*. CloudRaft. https://www.cloudraft.io/blog/monitoring-with-prometheus

Ronquillo, A., (2024, February 28). *Python's request library (guide)*. RealPython. https://realpython.com/python-requests/

Sajid, H. *PyCharm vs. Spyder: choosing the right Python ide*. (2023, September 15). Www.unite.ai. https://www.unite.ai/pycharm-vs-spyder-choosing-the-right-python-ide/

Singh, G. (2023, August 22). *Mastering microservices design patterns: a comprehensive guide*. Medium. https://vertisystem.medium.com/mastering-microservices-design-patterns-a-comprehensive-guide-d48564fd90c0

Singh, V. (2023, September 6). *Acid properties and how to implement acid properties in DBMS*. LinkedIn. https://www.linkedin.com/pulse/acid-properties-how-implement-dbms-vaishali-singh/

SQL create index statement. (n.d.). W3Schools. https://www.w3schools.com/sql/sql_create_index.asp

Star method. (2022). Mindtools.com. https://www.mindtools.com/ah3yoie/star-method

Thomas, D. (2023, February 10). *Using caching strategies to improve API performance*. Lonti.com; Toro Cloud Pty Ltd. https://www.lonti.com/blog/using-caching-strategies-to-improve-api-performance

Top 80+ data engineer interview questions and answers. (2019, October 24). Simplilearn. https://www.simplilearn.com/data-engineer-interview-questions-and-answers-article

Top 10 Python IDEs in 2024. (2024, January 23). GeeksForGeeks. https://www.geeksforgeeks.org/top-python-ide/

Top 11 microservices design patterns and how to choose. (2023). Codesee.io. https://www.codesee.io/learning-center/microservices-design-patterns

Urban, W., Rogowska, P. (2018, September) *The case study of bottlenecks identification for practical implementation to the theory of constraints*. ResearchGate. https://www.researchgate.net/publication/328337894_The_Case_Study_of_Bottlenecks_Identification_for_Practical_Implementation_to_the_Theory_of_Constraints

Using IDEs. (n.d.).Anaconda Inc. https://docs.anaconda.com/working-with-conda/ide-tutorials/

What is a restful API?. (n.d.). Amazon Web Services. https://aws.amazon.com/what-is/restful-api/

What is Apache Cassandra?. (n.d.). Apache. https://cassandra.apache.org/_/index.html

What is data bottleneck?. (2023). Dremio.com. https://www.dremio.com/wiki/data-bottleneck/

What is data pipeline: components, types, and use cases. (2022, May 17). AltexSoft. https://www.altexsoft.com/blog/data-pipeline-components-and-types/

What is network throughput? How to measure and improve it. (n.d.). NileSecure. https://nilesecure.com/network-management/what-is-network-throughput-how-to-measure-and-improve-it

Vasileva, I. (2021, January 14). *How to set up a data science project*. Medium. https://iskriyana.medium.com/how-to-set-up-a-data-science-project-27c3152f4f2a

Willems, K. (2022, December 12). *Pandas tutorial: DataFrames in Python*. Www.datacamp.com. https://www.datacamp.com/tutorial/pandas-tutorial-dataframe-python

Designing Data Intensive Applications

BOOK 2

Introduction

Imagine you're standing at a crowded train station, surrounded by the hum of bustling commuters, each with their own destination and timeline. The tracks span out in every direction, carrying passengers swiftly from one point to another with precision and efficiency. Now, picture these trains as streams of data racing through the digital landscape of your organization. Each piece of information holds potential insights, decisions, and actions waiting to be unlocked. Yet, without effective systems in place, this data remains like those travelers—stuck in limbo at the platform, going nowhere fast.

If you've ever tried to make sense of an overwhelming avalanche of data, only to find that your current systems are gasping to keep up, you're not alone. Today's data-driven environment demands more than just traditional data management practices; it requires innovative solutions that can process vast quantities of information in real time. This is no longer just a challenge for tech giants or global enterprises; it's an obstacle faced by every business bound by data.

Welcome to a world where stagnation isn't an option, where businesses are quite literally drowning in data. Every click, swipe, view, or transaction generates nuggets of data that could be the key to understanding customer behavior, operational efficiencies, market trends, or future innovations. However, the sheer volume and velocity of this data can cripple organizations that lack the infrastructure to convert it into actionable insights swiftly. Falling behind in this race isn't just about lost opportunities; it's about survival in an increasingly competitive landscape.

But here's the good news: Navigating the oceans of data doesn't have to feel like steering a rudderless ship. This book aims to equip you with the tools and knowledge to transform those torrents of data into streams of insight, laying the foundation for systems that not only meet today's demands but are poised to tackle tomorrow's challenges head-on. Whether you're building from scratch or seeking ways to scale existing infrastructures, you'll find guidance here tailored to both ends of the spectrum.

By embarking on this journey, you're setting yourself on a path that blends theory with practical application, ensuring what you learn can be immediately implemented. Our approach is designed to be hands-on, demystifying complex processes by bringing them down to earth in a way that's understandable yet sophisticated enough to make a real difference in your day-to-day work. You'll not only grasp the theoretical concepts behind data engineering but will also acquire tangible skills, enabling you to build scalable, efficient data systems that function effortlessly under real-world pressures.

So what's in store for you? Think of this book as a series of dynamic projects where each chapter builds upon the last, slicing through intricate themes with clarity and simplicity. We'll start by constructing fundamental distributed data pipelines, gradually moving on to orchestrating robust microservices that operate seamlessly within your architecture. By the end, you'll not just understand how these systems operate; you'll have crafted them with your own hands, ready to deploy on your terms.

Our exploration won't just stop at system creation. We'll dive deep into optimizing performance and maintaining scalability, dealing with the nuances of real-time processing methodologies, and ensuring that security and reliability are never compromised. With every turn of the page, you'll be closer to mastering the art of data engineering, ready to step confidently into roles that demand such expertise.

Whether you're an experienced data engineer, a software developer stepping into the data-rich world, or someone eyeing a career shift into data engineering, this book provides a comprehensive overview sprinkled with industry-relevant insights. For students, practitioners, and professionals alike, the lessons contained here speak directly to the core of your aspirations, merging technical rigor with genuine excitement for the field.

Why does this matter to you? Well, think of the possibilities: Efficient data systems not only enable faster decision-making but also drive innovation within your organization. They allow you to respond to market changes with agility, uncover hidden patterns, optimize operations, and ultimately, provide a better service or product to your clients. In short, they position you a step ahead, keeping your competitive edge sharp and defined.

In a rapidly evolving technological landscape, gaining mastery over data systems is akin to unlocking a new dimension of capabilities. It's about harnessing the full power of your data reservoir and turning it into a strategic asset that propels your success story forward. This book intends to guide you through that transformation, offering insights and techniques that bridge gaps and open doors.

So, as you commit to this adventure, prepare to step into a realm where data meets ingenuity, creating pathways that lead to unprecedented outcomes. You're not just learning to code or configure; you're redefining the boundaries of what's possible with data and reshaping perspectives in a way that echoes far beyond your immediate surroundings.

Grab your metaphorical ticket, board this train of knowledge, and let's set off on a quest to redefine how we interact with data in a world that never stands still. Your seat is booked, the engines are fired up, and your journey toward data-driven empowerment begins now.

Chapter 1

No-Nonsense Introduction—Building Data Systems That Work

Creating effective data systems presents both technical challenges and practical necessities. When you handle massive amounts of data or maintain real-time processing, a reliable system underpins data-driven operations. How can we build data systems that perform well under heavy loads? This requires combining speed and efficiency with modern technology, prioritizing user satisfaction. Through examining innovative frameworks and automation tools, this chapter will break down the complexity and provide practical insights.

To summarize, in this chapter, we will look at:

- Understanding the critical role of speed and efficiency in modern data systems.

- Identifying and implementing key performance metrics.

- Practical approaches to building scalable data pipelines.

- Real-world examples and hands-on implementations.

Importance of Speed and Efficiency in Modern Data Systems

Speed and efficiency are desirable traits in a data system. As users expect immediate access to information, real-time data processing is a key component for effective system design. A user navigates traffic using a navigation app with a five-minute delay. This creates the experience users face when data systems lack rapid processing. A data system that lags frustrates its users and can cost companies in terms of both money and resources.

The demand for real-time data continues growing across sectors. From financial services to healthcare and retail, organizations rely on swift data transactions and insights to drive decisions. In finance, stock trading relies on real-time data for split-second buy or sell decisions. The expectation: Users want zero latency. If a system can't keep up with this expectation, it risks losing customers to competitors who can deliver. Systems must exceed expectations to secure loyalty and trust from users who depend on accuracy and speed.

Real-World Impact Metrics

Performance Metric	Business Impact
Page Loading Time	User Retention
Query Response	Customer Satisfaction
System Downtime	Revenue Loss
Data Freshness	Decision Quality

Cost Implications of Inefficient Systems

When systems underperform, slow data systems reduce operational efficiency. They become bottlenecks, delaying decision-making and leading to poor outcomes due to outdated information. This inefficiency creates increased operational costs. Consider the costs of maintaining additional hardware to compensate for processing delays or loss of revenue when customers select competitors due to poor performance. Speed becomes more than a technical requirement and transforms into a critical business need. Companies that prioritize efficient systems reduce waste and improve their bottom line.

Cost Analysis Framework

Consider these key areas when evaluating system costs:

1. Direct Infrastructure Costs

   - hardware expenses

   - software licenses

   - maintenance fees

   - cloud service charges

2. Indirect Operational Costs

   - system downtime impact

   - lost productivity

   - customer churn rate

   - support team overhead

Impact on Competitive Advantage

Success depends on the speed of a company's data system. Organizations use quick data processing for creating better user experiences. Consider e-commerce platforms. Customers expect seamless browsing, instant transaction processing, and real-time inventory updates—all requiring fast underlying data systems. Efficient systems create happier customers, generating repeat business and brand advocacy. Timely and accurate data supports informed decision-making, allowing businesses to act swiftly in dynamic markets. Without responsiveness, companies risk falling behind, especially when competitors use their own efficient systems to offer superior services.

Market Position Assessment Guide

Track these metrics to measure your competitive position:

1. Performance Benchmarks

    ○ industry-standard response times

    ○ competitor system capabilities

    ○ market leader performance metrics

    ○ customer expectation surveys

2. Competitive Edge Indicators

    ○ customer retention rates

    ○ market share trends

    ○ feature adoption rates

    ○ user satisfaction scores

Technological Advancements Driving Efficiency

New software frameworks and automation tools change how data systems operate. These advancements create reduced processing latency, making it possible to handle data velocity without significant infrastructure strain. Modern frameworks help developers build systems that are reliable and scalable, handling growing data loads without compromising speed. Automation improves integration processes. Automated routine tasks reduce manual intervention, reducing errors and speeding up operations. The result is a smoother workflow that supports rapid responses to user demands and changing market conditions.

Technology Adoption Roadmap

Follow this structured approach when implementing new technologies:

Phase 1: Assessment

- evaluate current technology stack

- identify performance gaps

- research available solutions

- calculate implementation costs

Phase 2: Planning

- set clear adoption timelines

- define success metrics

- plan training programs

- create fallback strategies

Phase 3: Implementation

- start with pilot projects

- measure initial results

- gather user feedback

- adjust based on findings

Real-World Examples of Successful Implementations

Companies across various sectors have demonstrated the transformative power of efficient data systems:

1. **Netflix:** Their recommendation engine processes vast amounts of viewing data in real-time, providing personalized content suggestions that keep users engaged.

2. **Amazon:** Their inventory management system processes millions of transactions per second, ensuring accurate stock levels across global warehouses.

3. **Financial institutions:** High-frequency trading firms leverage ultra-low latency systems to execute trades in microseconds.

It's fascinating to observe how automation tools have taken center stage in reducing system integration issues. Tools like Docker, Kubernetes, and Apache Kafka have revolutionized the way applications communicate and process data. They provide the scaffolding necessary to deploy changes rapidly and ensure that systems remain agile under varying loads. When integrating these tools, companies can streamline their workflows, reduce latency, and enhance overall system reliability. This technological edge often distinguishes industry leaders from laggards, highlighting the pivotal role of strategic investments in technology.

Overview of Projects and Systems to Be Built

This book focuses on building real-world data systems through hands-on projects. This method simplifies theoretical concepts by applying them to practical situations, helping readers understand the theory and bring these ideas to life.

Project Variety

Let's examine the projects. Projects range from basic data ingestion systems to advanced real-time analytics. Readers work with both batch and real-time processing environments. Basic data ingestion includes setting up a pipeline that collects data from multiple sources, cleans it, and loads it into a database. Real-time analytics projects process streaming data in milliseconds to make data available for insights. This diversity creates a comprehensive experience, covering various aspects of data system construction.

Project Selection Guide

Consider these factors when choosing your first implementation project:

1. Complexity Levels

    ○ beginner: data ingestion pipelines

    ○ intermediate: real-time processing systems

    ○ advanced: distributed analytics platforms

2. Resource Requirements

    ○ team expertise needed

    ○ time investment

    ○ infrastructure demands

    ○ budget considerations

3. Business Impact

    ○ immediate value delivery

    ○ risk level

    ○ stakeholder benefits

    ○ learning opportunities

Incremental Learning Approach

The structure of our learning is incremental, meaning each project builds on the last. This method progressively introduces new concepts and challenges, mirroring real-life scenarios where complexity increases as you build your expertise. For instance, you might first learn to handle data at rest before moving to data in motion. Imagine first creating a simple batch processing system, then evolving it into a real-time system capable of handling live data streams. This step-by-step approach not only leads to mastery but also makes complex ideas more digestible.

Learning Path Framework

Structure your learning journey using this progressive approach:

1. Foundation Phase (1–2 months)

    ○ basic data processing concepts

- simple ETL pipelines

- data storage fundamentals

- basic monitoring skills

2. Intermediate Phase (2–3 months)

- real-time processing

- performance optimization

- error handling strategies

- scalability principles

3. Advanced Phase (3–4 months)

- distributed systems

- high-availability architectures

- advanced monitoring

- system optimization

Importance of Hands-On Experience

Given the dynamic nature of the tech world, having hands-on experience has never been more important. Theoretical knowledge can set strong foundations, but practical skills are what really set you apart in the workforce. Through these projects, you'll gain relevant, applicable skills, which significantly boost your employability. Just picture for a moment being able to showcase your ability to design a scalable data pipeline or automate a process that saves time and resources—skills highly valued by employers.

Practical Experience Checklist

Build your expertise systematically:

1. Essential Skills Development

        ○ data pipeline creation

        ○ system monitoring setup

        ○ performance tuning

        ○ troubleshooting procedures

2. Project Documentation

        ○ system architecture diagrams

        ○ performance benchmarks

        ○ implementation challenges

        ○ solution strategies

3. Portfolio Building

        ○ small-scale implementations

        ○ performance optimization cases

        ○ system scaling examples

        ○ problem-solving scenarios

Expected Outcomes From Projects

As we progress, you'll find that these projects aren't just exercises; they're portfolio pieces. After completing these projects, you will become proficient in designing and implementing data pipelines that operate both theoretically and efficiently in practice. The projects show technical capabilities, useful for potential employers or clients. From students, professionals transitioning into data engineering, or seasoned developers looking to expand their skill set, these projects demonstrate expertise.

Skills Development Matrix

Track your progress across these key competencies:

1. Technical Proficiency

   - system design principles

   - performance optimization

   - scalability implementation

   - monitoring and maintenance

2. Business Impact

   - cost optimization achieved

   - performance improvements

   - user satisfaction increases

   - resource utilization gains

3. Professional Growth

   - portfolio development

   - case study creation

   - documentation skills

   - problem-solving abilities

Learning Best Practices

To encourage effective learning, let's get a little into the foundational practices that guide these projects. Start with smaller, manageable projects to gain confidence. As you grasp the basics, gradually take on more challenging ones. Use documentation and community forums when faced with roadblocks; these resources are goldmines of collective knowledge and often offer solutions that aren't immediately obvious. Building a habit of iteration—constantly revising and optimizing your projects—will also improve your skills remarkably.

Learning Strategy Guide

Optimize your learning journey:

1. Study Approach

    ○ daily practice sessions

    ○ weekly project reviews

    ○ monthly skill assessments

    ○ quarterly goal setting

2. Resource Utilization

    ○ documentation libraries

    ○ community forums

    ○ expert blogs

    ○ technical workshops

3. Progress Tracking

    ○ skills inventory

    ○ project completion rates

    ○ understanding assessments

    ○ practical application success

Technology Stack Overview

Another aspect is learning commonly used tools and technologies. Using frameworks like Apache Kafka for stream processing and databases like MongoDB for flexible storage, understanding these tools improves technology selection. Each tool has strengths and trade-offs, and hands-on experience supports informed decisions in real-world applications.

Learning Philosophy

Remember, the beauty of diving into hands-on projects lies in the experience itself. Mistakes are just stepping stones to understanding. Each error pushes you to search deeper, discover new methodologies, and refine your approach. Embrace these opportunities to grow; learning happens most effectively when you're deeply engaged in the problem-solving process.

Action Plan Template

Implement your learning with this structured approach:

1. Immediate Actions (First Week)

    ○ system assessment

    ○ goal setting

    ○ resource gathering

    ○ schedule planning

2. Short-Term Goals (First Month)

    ○ basic implementation

    ○ initial monitoring setup

    ○ performance baseline

    ○ first optimization round

3. Long-Term Strategy (Six Months)

    ○ advanced system features

- o performance refinement

- o portfolio development

- o expertise demonstration

Key Takeaways

- Speed and efficiency in data systems are crucial for meeting user expectations and maintaining a competitive advantage, with slow performance directly impacting user satisfaction and business opportunities.

- Real-time data processing is essential across industries, particularly for time-sensitive operations like financial transactions and inventory management.

- Fast, efficient systems create a positive feedback loop—they improve user satisfaction while building a strong foundation for business growth and long-term success.

Chapter 2

Quick Foundations—Core Building Blocks of Data Systems

Scaling data systems stands as a fundamental challenge in technology. Like constructing skyscrapers, data systems need solid architectural principles. Three architectural principles power modern data engineering: scalability, replication, and sharding. These concepts form the backbone of reliable, high-performance systems. Mastering these principles helps you build systems that handle heavy loads and stay available during outages. This chapter examines each principle in detail. We start with scaling patterns, analyzing vertical and horizontal approaches and their best applications. Learn from Facebook and Google's real-world implementations for managing massive data loads.

Here, we will look at:

- Basic understanding of distributed systems.

- Familiarity with database concepts.

- Access to a development environment.

- Design scalable data systems using both vertical and horizontal approaches.

- Implement replication strategies based on specific use cases.

- Create effective sharding solutions for large datasets.

- Evaluate trade-offs between different scaling approaches.

Understanding Scalability, Replication, and Sharding

Understanding how key system components interact creates the foundation for reliable data architectures. These three pillars—scalability, replication, and sharding—define successful data system design.

Scalability: Building Systems That Grow

Scalability measures how well a system handles growing workloads. Think of it as managing seating at a restaurant—you can use bigger tables or add more tables. Scalability comes in two forms:

Vertical vs. Horizontal Scaling

Vertical scaling, often referred to as "scaling up," involves adding more power to existing machines. This could mean upgrading CPUs, adding RAM, or enhancing storage capabilities. Although it sounds straightforward, there's a catch. There's only so much you can upgrade before hitting physical or cost limits. On the other hand, horizontal scaling, or "scaling out," spreads the load across more machines. Imagine adding more tables instead of just expanding one. This method is often more flexible and cost-effective, especially for large-scale applications. However, horizontal scaling brings its own set of challenges, such as ensuring that distributed systems work harmoniously.

Scaling Approaches Detailed Comparison

Aspect	Vertical Scaling	Horizontal Scaling
Initial Cost	Higher upfront investment	Lower initial investment
Long-Term Cost	Exponential cost growth	Linear cost growth

Implementation Complexity	Lower	Higher
Application Changes	Minimal to none	Often required
Downtime Risk	Higher during upgrades	Lower, rolling updates possible
Performance Ceiling	Hardware limited	Theoretically unlimited
Data Consistency	Easier to maintain	More complex
Fault Tolerance	Single point of failure	Better fault tolerance
Geographic Distribution	Limited	Excellent

Real-World Scalability Examples

Facebook and Google's data management strategies showcase practical scaling applications. These tech giants spread operations across global server networks instead of focusing on single-server upgrades. Their implementations guide data engineers in building high-performance systems.

Replication: Ensuring Data Availability

Replication keeps systems running during peak periods, such as when e-commerce platforms handle major sales. It works by maintaining data copies across multiple servers. When one server fails, others continue operations without interruption. This happens through two main approaches: synchronous and asynchronous replication.

Replication Method Selection Guide

Factor	Synchronous	Asynchronous
Data Consistency	Immediate	Evenly Consistent

Performance Impact	Higher	Lower
Network Dependency	Critical	Less Critical
Use Cases	Financial Systems, Critical Transactions	Content Delivery, Analytics
Recovery Time	Faster	May Need Reconciliation
Resource Usage	Higher	Lower
Geographic Distribution	Limited by Latency	Excellent

Synchronous vs. Asynchronous Replication

In synchronous replication, systems maintain data consistency by waiting for all nodes to confirm the transaction before considering it complete. Although this keeps your data consistently accurate, it can slow things down. In contrast, asynchronous replication doesn't wait. It lets transactions proceed and updates nodes later, which speeds up processes but creates potential temporary inconsistencies.

Replication Strategy Assessment Framework

1. Requirements Analysis

- Business Requirements

    - data consistency needs

    - acceptable latency

    - recovery time objectives

    - geographic distribution

- Technical Constraints

- network bandwidth

- storage capacity

- processing power

- budget limitations

2. Strategy Selection Matrix

- Choose Synchronous

  - zero data loss is required

  - transactions are critical

  - network latency is low

  - resources are adequate

- Choose Asynchronous

  - some lag is acceptable

  - performance is priority

  - network is unreliable

  - cost optimization needed

Both approaches work best in specific scenarios. Consider financial systems, where data consistency remains critical, establishing synchronous replication as standard practice. Meanwhile, systems focused on speed often use asynchronous methods, accepting occasional discrepancies for faster outputs.

When implementing replication, organizations should understand their needs and trade-offs. Companies like Netflix implement replication so users worldwide can stream without interruption, even when data centers face outages. This represents the balance between fault tolerance and performance in data engineering.

Replication Strategies in Practice

Organizations must consider several factors when implementing replication:

- data consistency requirements

- geographic distribution of users

- acceptable latency thresholds

- resource availability and costs

Replication Implementation Checklist

Phase	Tasks	Validation Criteria
Planning	Infrastructure assessment, Network analysis	Resource availability confirmed
Design	Topology selection, Failover strategy	Architecture documents approved
Implementation	Node setup, Configuration	System tests passed
Testing	Load testing, Failover testing	Performance metrics met
Monitoring	Metrics setup, Alert configuration	Monitoring dashboard active
Maintenance	Backup procedures, Update strategy	Maintenance schedule established

Sharding: Breaking Down Big Data

Lastly, let's talk about sharding—a technique that breaks big data into smaller, manageable chunks spread across multiple servers. Think of sharding like slicing a pizza into pieces, making it easier to handle and serve each slice without overwhelming a single plate. But not just any slicing will do. The secret sauce here is choosing effective sharding keys that determine how data is divided.

Sharding Key Selection Criteria

Criteria	Description	Impact
Cardinality	Number of unique values	Affects distribution balance
Distribution	Value spread pattern	Determines shard sizes
Query Patterns	How data is accessed	Influences cross-shard queries
Growth Pattern	How data grows over time	Affects long-term balance
Business Logic	Application requirements	Determines access patterns

Sharding Strategy Framework

I. Reimplementation Analysis

(a). Data Assessment

- total data volume

- growth rate

- access patterns

- query complexity

(b). Infrastructure Requirements

- number of shards needed

- storage per shard

- network capacity

- processing power

II. Implementation Considerations

(a). Architecture Decisions

- shard key selection

- rebalancing strategy

- backup approach

- monitoring setup

(b). Operational Procedures

- shard migration process

- maintenance windows

- emergency procedures

- performance monitoring

Facebook again is an excellent case study, massively relying on sharding to cope with its endless streams of user data. Through adept sharding techniques, they maintain quick response times and efficient data retrieval, illustrating how critical strategic sharding is for performance enhancement.

Sharding Implementation Phases

Phase	Activities	Deliverables	Success Metrics
Analysis	Data profiling, Requirements gathering	Requirements document	Completion of analysis
Design	Architecture planning, Shard key selection	Technical design	Design approval
Setup	Infrastructure preparation, Tool configuration	Working environment	System readiness
Migration	Data transfer, Application updates	Migrated system	Data integrity
Testing	Performance testing, Failover testing	Test results	Meeting SLAs
Production	Deployment, Monitoring setup	Live system	Performance metrics

Sharding Best Practices

When implementing sharding, consider

- data access patterns

- shard key selection criteria

- cross-shard query optimization

- load balancing strategies

Risk Assessment Matrix

Risk Category	Potential Issues	Mitigation Strategies	Priority
Performance	Hot shards, Slow queries	Rebalancing, Key optimization	High
Availability	Shard failures, Network issues	Redundancy, Failover	Critical
Maintenance	Rebalancing overhead, Updates	Automated tools, Planning	Medium
Scalability	Growth limitations, Hotspots	Flexible architecture, Monitoring	High

Industry Challenges and Solutions

All said, industry challenges surrounding scalability, replication, and sharding remain prevalent. Data systems continuously evolve, requiring creative solutions to persistent problems. Companies often find themselves in uncharted waters, experimenting and pioneering methods to push boundaries further.

Challenge	Impact	Solution Approaches	Industry Examples
Data Volume Growth	Performance degradation	Progressive sharding	Facebook's user data
Global Distribution	Latency issues	Regional replication	Netflix's content delivery

System Complexity	Maintenance overhead	Microservices architecture	Spotify's service model
Cost Management	Operating expenses	Hybrid scaling strategies	Twitter's infrastructure
Real-time Processing	Processing delays	Stream processing	LinkedIn's feed system

Take Spotify's journey, for instance. As they expanded globally, tackling scalability was non-negotiable. But when creatively implementing microservices architecture combined with agile scaling methods, they made sure music lovers worldwide experienced uninterrupted beats, no matter how crowded the dance floor got.

Strategic Implementation Framework

I. Challenge Assessment

(a). Business Impact Analysis

- revenue implications

- user experience effects

- market competitiveness

- operational efficiency

(b). Technical Impact Analysis

- system performance

- resource utilization

- maintenance requirements

- security implications

II. Solution Development

(a). Short-term Strategies

- immediate fixes

- quick wins

- risk mitigation

- performance optimization

(b). Long-term Planning

- architecture evolution

- scalability roadmap

- technology adoption

- resource planning

Hands-On Introduction to Distributed Data Pipelines

Building distributed data pipelines moves information across multiple systems. Understanding how distributed systems work shapes pipeline design. In pipeline construction, engineers balance trade-offs between consistency, availability, and partition tolerance—concepts defined by the CAP theorem. This theorem states you can't have all three simultaneously, leading to strategic decisions matching system priorities with specific application needs.

Component	Function	Considerations	Implementation Options
Ingestion	Data collection	Volume, variety	Kafka, Kinesis
Processing	Transformation	Latency, complexity	Spark, Flink
Storage	Data persistence	Durability, access	HDFS, S3
Analysis	Insight generation	Performance, accuracy	Presto, Redshift

The CAP Theorem Trade-Offs

When systems need real-time data updates where users see the most current information, you can prioritize consistency and partition tolerance, accepting some potential downtime. Or, if user experience needs high availability, compromising on immediate consistency becomes an option. Each choice determines how your data pipeline performs under different conditions. These decisions shape the architecture of distributed systems.

CAP Theorem Decision Matrix

Priority	Consistency + Availability	Consistency + Partition Tolerance	Availability + Partition Tolerance
Use Case	Local transactions	Critical financial systems	Content delivery networks
Trade-off	Network partition handling	Availability during failures	Data consistency
Example System	Traditional RDBMS	Banking systems	NoSQL databases

Implementation Cost	Medium	High	Medium
Operational Complexity	Low	High	Medium

Essential Pipeline Components

Let's break down the anatomy of a solid data pipeline. These pipelines typically involve four key stages: data ingestion, processing, storage, and analytics. From sourcing raw data (ingestion), using real-time or batch processing frameworks to mold and transform it, storing it efficiently, to finally running analytics to extract useful insights—each stage is important. Here, open-source tools like Apache Kafka and Apache Flink can be quite relevant. Kafka acts like a reliable courier, adeptly handling large volumes of event data for real-time streams. Meanwhile, Flink provides sophisticated processing capabilities, enabling low-latency data processing suitable for instant actions or analytics.

Key Pipeline Stages

1. Data Ingestion

    o source identification

    o data collection methods

    o input validation

2. Processing

    o batch vs. real-time

    o transformation rules

    o data cleansing

3. Storage

    o database selection

- data modeling

- retention policies

4. Analytics

- reporting requirements

- visualization needs

- insight generation

Hands-On Project Implementation

To understand the mechanics of setting up a distributed pipeline, start with a simple project. Building a pilot project helps you experiment and learn. Try setting up a basic pipeline that collects social media posts via an API, analyzes this data with Flink for sentiment analysis, and stores the output in a database for querying and visualization. This project reveals common pitfalls, such as latency issues or unexpected data spikes, and shows troubleshooting techniques for each challenge.

Project Setup Guidelines

When starting your first pipeline project, consider:

- defining clear project objectives

- selecting appropriate tools

- setting up monitoring

- establishing error handling

Real-World Implementation Examples

Large companies demonstrate how distributed data pipelines handle large-scale analytics. Netflix's data pipeline handles billions of events daily, sourced from users worldwide. Through distributed systems and data centers across regions, Netflix maintains seamless streaming experiences through dynamic content distribution matching user location and demand.

Google provides another compelling example with its search engine infrastructure. A massive distributed setup supports real-time indexing, processing thousands of queries per second while continuously updating its database. Here, the challenges of partitioning data and ensuring quick retrieval times are tackled by meticulous engineering and innovations in distributed computing practices.

When exploring what industry giants do, you gain actionable insights into applying similar strategies in your projects, learning to anticipate potential challenges and devise creative solutions. These real-world examples are an inspiration and can be used as practical guides, giving you a blueprint of what's possible with distributed data pipelines when thoughtfully architected.

Industry Case Studies

1. Netflix's Global Content Delivery

   ○ billions of daily events

   ○ global data center strategy

   ○ dynamic content distribution

2. Google's Search Infrastructure

   ○ real-time indexing

   ○ query processing

   ○ distributed computing practices

Best Practices and Common Pitfalls

When building distributed data pipelines, keep in mind:

Best Practices

- start small and scale gradually

- implement comprehensive monitoring

- plan for failure scenarios

- document system architecture

Common Pitfalls to Avoid

- overlooking data validation

- insufficient error handling

- poor monitoring implementation

- inadequate scaling planning

Key Takeaways

- The chapter introduced three fundamental concepts for data system design: scalability (both vertical and horizontal), replication (synchronous and asynchronous), and sharding—illustrated through real-world examples from companies like Facebook and Google.

- Engineers must understand the trade-offs between different scaling approaches: vertical (adding power to one machine) versus horizontal (distributing across multiple machines), with horizontal scaling offering more flexibility for large-scale operations.

- Replication strategies involve a critical choice between synchronous methods (prioritizing data accuracy) and asynchronous methods (prioritizing speed), with the selection depending on specific use case requirements.

Chapter 3

Building a Real-Time Data Pipeline—Step-by-Step Implementation

Creating a real-time data pipeline establishes a seamless flow of information, letting businesses respond immediately to changes or patterns. The capacity to process data in real time strengthens a company's competitive edge. Companies can adjust marketing strategies based on current consumer behaviors or optimize inventory levels with feedback from sales trends. This agility is essential for any data-driven industry. Building these pipelines requires understanding data collection, processing, and output.

So, here, you will learn:

- Understand the fundamentals of real-time data pipelines.

- Master the implementation of real-time processing systems.

- Learn to deploy pipelines using Infrastructure as Code (IaC).

Significance of Real-Time Processing and Its Challenges

The current digital acceleration demands instant data processing, which helps companies compete better and improve customer satisfaction. Companies using real-time data eliminate delayed information delivery and turn insights into actions.

Industry Application Table

Industry	Key Applications		Business Value
Retail	Inventory management, Customer behavior	Performance Metrics	Increased sales, Better stock control
Finance	Fraud detection, Trading	Processing speed < 100ms	Risk reduction, Trading advantages
Sports	Live analytics, Fan engagement	Microsecond latency	Enhanced viewer experience
Healthcare	Patient monitoring, Resource allocation	Real-time statistics	Improved patient outcomes

Practice Exercise: Industry Analysis

Identify your industry's specific needs:

- primary data sources

- required processing speed

- key business metrics

Understanding Real-Time Use Cases

A retail company using real-time data analytics can track consumer behavior—tracking what and when customers buy, and accurately predicting future purchasing patterns. Real-time analysis improves personalized offers, adjusts inventory, and refines marketing campaigns. This creates better customer experiences, increasing brand loyalty and market share.

Use Case Template

Project Name: [Your Pipeline Name]

Industry Vertical: [Your Industry]

Primary Objectives

- [Objective 1]

- [Objective 2]

- [Objective 3]

Key Requirements

- data sources:

- processing speed:

- volume expectations:

- compliance needs:

Implementation Analysis Framework

I. Use Case Requirements

(a). Data Collection Points

- customer interactions

- transaction records

- inventory levels

- website analytics

(b). Processing Requirements

- latency tolerance

- data volume expectations

- accuracy requirements

- compliance needs

II. System Architecture Considerations

(a). Infrastructure Components

- data ingestion layers

- processing engines

- storage solutions

- analytics platforms

Impact on Decision-Making

Real-time data processing creates adaptability across numerous industries, speeding up decision-making. Watch an airline apply real-time data to modify flights based on weather patterns and passenger needs. This leads to fewer delays and efficient routes, reducing costs and improving service quality. Also, financial institutions implementing real-time analytics detect fraudulent activities instantly, protecting assets and building trust with their customers.

Decision-Making Impact Matrix

Decision Type	Traditional Approach	Real-Time Approach	Business Impact
Inventory Management	Daily updates	Instant tracking	30% cost reduction
Price Optimization	Weekly adjustments	Dynamic pricing	25% revenue increase

Risk Assessment	Periodic review	Continuous monitoring	40% risk reduction
Customer Service	Reactive response	Proactive engagement	50% satisfaction increase

Practice Exercise: Impact Analysis

Using your organization as an example:

(a). Current decision-making process

- process time

- data sources

- key bottlenecks

(b). Proposed real-time approach

- expected improvements

- required changes

- anticipated challenges

Within professional sports, real-time data processing transforms both game analysis and viewer engagement. Major sports leagues use sophisticated systems to capture and process thousands of data points per second, tracking player movements and ball trajectories. During a basketball game, real-time analytics systems process player performance metrics like shooting percentages, court positioning, and defensive effectiveness to update team strategies and broadcast statistics immediately.

Sports Analytics Implementation Guide

I. Data Collection Systems

(a). Physical Metrics

- player positioning

- movement patterns

- performance indicators

- equipment telemetry

(b). Game Statistics

- scoring patterns

- team formations

- strategy effectiveness

- player interactions

II. Real-Time Analysis Requirements

(a). Processing Needs

- sub-second latency

- multiple data streams

- complex calculations

- visualization requirements

Implementation Checklist
- Data Collection System Setup

  - physical metrics configuration

  - game statistics integration

  - real-time feed verification

- Analysis Requirements

  - latency specifications

  - processing capacity planning

  - visualization requirements

Real-time data processing surpasses basic scorekeeping; modern systems connect with broadcasting networks, improving live commentary with instant statistical context, and update dynamic graphics systems showing game progress through visualizations. This benefits fans who engage with live games through mobile applications offering real-time stats, to track their favorite players' performance, participate in live prediction games, and make fantasy sports decisions based on instant information. Real-time data processing changes sports from a purely spectator experience into an interactive, data-rich entertainment platform supporting coaches in tactical decisions and fans wanting more engagement with the game.

Challenges of Implementing Real-Time Pipelines

However, achieving real-time capabilities isn't devoid of challenges. One significant hurdle is ensuring system stability while processing vast amounts of data at lightning speed. Maintaining data consistency in such dynamic conditions requires solid architecture and sophisticated algorithms capable of handling sudden influxes of information without compromising the integrity of data streams.

Implementation Challenges Overview

Challenge Category	Technical Impact	Business Impact	Mitigation Strategy
Data Volume	Processing overhead	Delayed insights	Distributed processing
System Stability	Service disruptions	Revenue loss	Redundant architecture
Data Consistency	Incorrect analytics	Poor decisions	Strong validation

| **Integration** | System complexity | Higher costs | Standardized protocols |

Challenge Mitigation Exercise

For each challenge in your environment:

Challenge #1:

Impact:

Mitigation Strategy:

Success Metrics:

Continue this for all the challenges.

Another technical challenge revolves around ensuring low-latency communication across diverse systems. As businesses grow, integrating multiple data sources becomes necessary, yet this integration must occur seamlessly. Any delay in data transmission not only risks outdated insights but also hampers the proactive response capabilities that define real-time success. To overcome this, state-of-the-art technologies need to be employed to reduce latency and optimize throughput.

Risk Assessment Matrix

Risk Factor	Probability	Impact	Mitigation Steps	Priority
System Overload	High	Critical	Auto-scaling, Load-balancing	Immediate
Data Loss	Medium	Severe	Backup systems, Redundancy	High
Latency Issues	High	Major	Edge computing, Caching	High

Integration Failures	Medium	Moderate	API monitoring, Fallbacks	Medium

Data-to-Insight Time Reduction

The transformation from raw data to actionable insights has seen dramatic acceleration through real-time processing capabilities. Where traditional batch processing methods typically introduced delays of hours or even days, modern real-time systems have reduced this window to milliseconds. Say, a major e-commerce platform, now processes customer behavior data within 50 milliseconds of user actions, allowing instantaneous personalization of shopping experiences. This reduction in data-to-insight latency has proven particularly valuable in high-stakes environments—such as stock trading platforms that analyze market movements and execute trades within microseconds or manufacturing facilities that adjust production parameters in real-time based on quality control metrics, resulting in defect rate reductions of up to 45%.

Processing Time Analysis Framework

I. Performance Metrics

(a). Processing Stages

- data ingestion time

- processing duration

- analysis completion

- insight delivery

(b). Optimization Targets

- current latency

- desired latency

- bottleneck identification

- improvement goals

II. System Optimization

(a). Technical Improvements

- hardware upgrades

- software optimization

- architecture refinement

- pipeline streamlining

Performance Optimization Template

Current State

- ingestion latency

- processing time

- analysis duration

- insight delivery

Target State

- desired latency

- processing improvements

- analysis optimization

- delivery enhancement

Action Items

- technical upgrades

- software optimization

- architecture changes

Strategic Operational Adjustments

Companies using real-time data reshape their operational dynamics through adjustments. Many modern logistics companies use dynamic routing systems that continuously analyze traffic patterns, weather conditions, and delivery priorities, recalculating optimal routes for thousands of vehicles. Energy utilities implement real-time grid management systems to balance power distribution based on consumption patterns, weather conditions, and renewable energy. These adjustments produce documented improvements, with companies reporting operational cost reductions of 15–30% and customer satisfaction increases of up to 40% through consistent service delivery.

Agile Integration

Combining real-time data processing and agile methodologies builds a new standard in business operations. Organizations shift from traditional sprint-based decision-making to continuous adaptation models, where data-driven insights start immediate responses to market changes. Development teams integrate real-time monitoring into their CI/CD pipelines, allowing automatic detection and resolution of issues before they impact end-users. Real-time agile speeds up the feedback loop between development and production environments, reducing the average time to implement critical changes from days to hours. Companies using these integrated real-time agile practices report up to 70% faster time-to-market for new features and a 60% reduction in post-deployment incidents.

Future Trends in Real-Time Processing

In the future, trends show machine learning and edge computing advance real-time data processing. Machine learning models, especially those at the edge, execute predictive data analysis closer to the source of information. Consider autonomous vehicles that rely on immediate data processing for split-second decision-making. The combination of edge computing and machine learning helps vehicles analyze surroundings quickly and react safely, improving safety and efficiency.

IoT uses real-time processing, and with machine learning, it changes conventional practices. Smart cities apply real-time data to manage traffic flows, optimize energy consumption, and improve public transportation systems for more sustainable urban environments.

Organizations should focus on adopting and refining real-time data strategies matching innovation. Following technological advancements allows businesses to use predictive analytics and computational power to extract valuable insights from growing data generated daily.

Deploying Real-Time Pipelines with Infrastructure as Code Tools

Deploying real-time data pipelines, Infrastructure as Code (IaC) tools such as Terraform and AWS CloudFormation transform workflow efficiency for data engineers. These tools streamline the management and deployment of infrastructure. They maintain consistency across environments and boost collaboration among team members when building large-scale, data-intensive applications.

Infrastructure as Code fundamentally changes infrastructure management. It replaces manual processes with code-based configuration, reducing human error and providing a standardized framework. This establishes infrastructure consistency across development, testing, and production environments. As technical professionals learn data engineering, mastering IaC improves infrastructure control, freeing teams for application development instead of environment configurations.

Infrastructure as Code Comparison

Feature	Terraform	CloudFormation	Pulumi
Language	HCL	YALM/JSON	Multiple
Cloud Support	Multi-cloud	AWS-specific	Multi-cloud

Learning Curve	Moderate	Moderate	Varies
State Management	Built-in	AWS-managed	Built-in
Community Support	Extensive	AWS-focused	Growing

Deployment Strategy Framework

I. Infrastructure Planning

(a). Environment Specifications

- development requirements

- staging configuration

- production architecture

- disaster recovery setup

(b). Resource Management

- compute resources

- storage requirements

- network configuration

- security measures

II. Implementation Process

(a). Deployment Phases

- initial setup

- testing procedures

- validation steps

- production rollout

Using Terraform for Real-Time Pipelines

Understanding Terraform is a popular choice for creating modular and reusable pipeline structures in the cloud. Terraform lets engineers define infrastructure using a high-level configuration language. This method helps build, change, and version infrastructure with precision. Through modules, engineers package and reuse sets of resources, positioning Terraform as ideal for managing complex architectures needing scalability and flexibility.

When setting up a new real-time data pipeline, Terraform simplifies defining reusable components like network setups or compute instances shared across projects. This modularity speeds up deployment times and reduces errors since tested components avoid rewriting from scratch. IaC allows teams to experiment, iterate, and optimize their pipeline architectures, meeting modern data processing demands.

Terraform Component Organization

Component Type	Purpose	Dependencies	Management Level
Core Infrastructure	Base setup	None	Foundation
Data Processing	Stream handling	Core Infrastructure	Service
Storage Solutions	Data persistence	Core infrastructure	Service
Monitoring Tools	System oversight	All components	Operations
Security Controls	Access management	All components	Security

Terraform Practice Exercise

Create a basic configuration

1. Provide block:

   ○ [your code here]

 2. Resource block:

   ○ [your code here]

 3. Variable definitions:

   ○ [your code here]

Test your configuration

- syntax validation

- plan review

- apply test

Terraform Code Examples

Building real-time pipelines with Terraform needs specific configurations for reliable deployment. Start by defining the provider block, which specifies the cloud platform and authentication details. For real-time processing, engineers configure compute resources like AWS EC2 instances or managed Kubernetes clusters, paired with message queuing services such as Apache Kafka or Amazon MSK.

A modular design pattern in Terraform excels at organizing real-time pipeline components. Each element—data ingestion, processing, and storage—works in separate modules. A data ingestion module contains configurations for Apache Kafka clusters, including broker setups, topic configurations, and security protocols. In parallel, a processing module specifies stream processing resources using Apache Flink or Apache Spark Streaming, with auto-scaling policies and monitoring setups.

Utilizing CloudFormation for AWS Deployment

Exploring AWS CloudFormation, another tool that integrates with AWS services for deploying real-time pipelines. AWS CloudFormation helps developers use JSON or YAML templates to create and provision AWS infrastructure. This integration offers an advantage for organizations using AWS services, letting them manage their resources in a uniform, predictable manner.

Using CloudFormation, developers set up application ecosystems combining storage, networking, and serverless functions. Writing templates after configuring and optimizing an environment, engineers replicate it quickly. This makes your real-time data pipelines run consistently and accurately, handling large volumes of data without manual intervention. This helps students and practitioners enter real-world scenarios where CloudFormation expertise can accelerate career growth.

CloudFormation Implementation

Integration with AWS Kinesis forms the backbone of many real-time processing implementations in CloudFormation. A comprehensive setup typically begins with Kinesis Data Streams for data ingestion, configured with appropriate shard counts based on expected throughput. This integrates seamlessly with Kinesis Data Analytics for real-time processing and Kinesis Data Firehose for data delivery to various AWS storage services.

Resource Planning Matrix

Resource Type	Scaling Needs	Cost Impact	Performance Requirements
Compute	Auto-scaling	Variable	Low latency processing
Storage	Elastic growth	Usage-based	High throughput
Networking	Load balanced	Fixed + Variable	High bandwidth
Memory	Cache-driven	Usage-based	Quick access time

Template configurations for real-time processing in CloudFormation use a layered structure. The foundation layer creates networking components, including VPCs, subnets, and security groups supporting real-time data flow. The processing layer sets up resources for stream processing, such as Kinesis applications or managed Apache Flink clusters. The storage layer configures destinations like Amazon S3 for processed data, while the monitoring layer implements CloudWatch metrics and alarms for real-time processing performance.

Version control in CloudFormation stacks needs careful change management. Teams implement a staged deployment strategy, using nested stacks to manage complex infrastructure components. This method supports isolated testing of changes and simplified rollback procedures. Changes to processing components can undergo testing independently without affecting the pipeline infrastructure.

Best Practices for Infrastructure as Code

Let's now have a look at how we can implement best practices in documentation, testing, and naming conventions to strengthen IaC management. Infrastructure code documentation guides teams. Clear, comprehensive documentation enables seasoned engineers and newcomers to understand the architecture and underlying logic. This supports teams updating or scaling systems, keeping changes accurately reflected and communicated.

Testing infrastructure code prevents deployment issues. Automated testing catches configuration errors early, saving time and preventing costly redeployments. Tools like Terratest run automated tests against Terraform code, confirming everything works before reaching production.

Knowledge Check

1. What are the three most critical components of your real-time pipeline?

2. How will you address the top challenges in your implementation?

3. What metrics will you use to measure success?

Additional Resources

- official documentation links

- community forums

- reference architectures

- tool-specific guides

Key Takeaways

- Real-time data processing enables quick decision-making and improved customer satisfaction across industries, with applications ranging from retail to financial services.

- Successful implementation of real-time data pipelines requires addressing key challenges, particularly system stability and low-latency communication, to maintain data integrity.

- Infrastructure as Code (IaC) tools like Terraform and AWS CloudFormation play a crucial role in automating infrastructure management, reducing manual errors, and ensuring consistency.

Chapter 4

Optimizing for Speed—Batch and Real-Time Processing

Data processing speed relies on two major methods: batch and real-time processing. These techniques drive modern data engineering, matching unique demands and providing different benefits. Consider how batch processing resembles a slow but steady assembly line, handling large amounts of data at once. Meanwhile, real-time processing functions as a conveyor belt, quickly dealing with data as it comes in. Both have their strengths, which influence implementation decisions. This mirrors choosing between preparing a meal all at once or cooking quick snacks—each works best depending on specific needs and timing requirements.

In this chapter, we will

- compare batch and real-time processing approaches.

- master batch ETL system implementation.

- optimize data processing pipelines.

- implement effective monitoring strategies.

Implementing Batch ETL Systems

Beginning with batch extract transform load (ETL) systems, start by choosing an appropriate ETL tool. This decision affects the efficiency and scalability of your data processing workflows. Prioritize scalability in your considerations. As datasets grow, maintaining performance levels becomes critical. Select tools that offer scalability options and evaluate their community support and documentation. An active community becomes a key resource for troubleshooting common issues and sharing best practices.

Tool Comparison

Comparing features is a great way to start. Tools like Apache NiFi, Talend, or Microsoft Azure Data Factory provide unique strengths—some excel in ease of integration, while others offer advanced data transformation capabilities.

ETL Tool Evaluation Template

System Requirements

- data volume capacity

- integration needs

- security requirements

- scalability expectations

Tool Assessment

- features match

- community support

- documentation quality

- integration capabilities

Integration Guidance

Integrating ETL tools into existing architectures requires specific analysis. Start by checking the tool's compatibility with your current data sources and targets. Enterprise environments use multiple database systems, file formats, and APIs—your tool should connect with these endpoints. With legacy systems, choose ETL tools that provide native connectors or custom adapter capabilities.

Different scenarios also need different implementation strategies. With real-time data needs, select tools that offer both batch and micro-batch processing capabilities. For cloud-native environments, choose tools with cloud service integration and elastic scaling features. In on-premises deployments, select tools that provide resource management and operate within existing network security constraints.

Integration Checklist

- source system compatibility

- target system compatibility

- authentication requirements

- encryption standards

- performance benchmarks

Designing Batch Processing Workflows

After choosing a tool, designing your batch-processing workflow begins. Focus on optimizing every part of the process. Partitioning splits large datasets into smaller, manageable chunks based on specific criteria like time or geography. This strategy boosts performance and makes error tracking and recovery easier. Implement modularity in your design—breaking workflows into components supports maintenance and scalability. Like modular components, you can replace or upgrade individual pieces without rebuilding the whole structure.

Practical Exercise: Workflow Design

Design a basic batch-processing workflow

- Identify data sources

    - Source 1: (type, volume, frequency)

    - Source 2: (type, volume, frequency)

- Define process steps

    - Step 1:

    - Step 2:

    - Step 3:

Job Dependencies

Defining and managing job dependencies needs careful orchestration for efficient data flow. First, map out critical paths in your data pipeline, identifying which jobs must complete before others can begin. Add checkpoint mechanisms to track job progress and create reliable recovery points. In a financial reporting pipeline, daily transaction processing must be completed before aggregation jobs can begin, while data quality checks run in parallel with initial extraction processes.

Workflow optimization targets reducing pipeline bottlenecks. Use smart dependency management to group related tasks and allow independent job streams to run concurrently. Apply fan-out/fan-in patterns for processes that run in parallel, such as processing different geographical regions independently before final consolidation.

Handling Data Quality and Validation

Let's examine data quality and validation. High-quality data supports accurate analysis and insights. Data validation checks confirm the data meets business requirements before the transformation stage begins. Using schema validation, data type checks, and consistency validations maintains clean data through your pipeline.

Error-handling strategies matter equally. If errors occur—and they will—the system must recover quickly. Create a plan for retry mechanisms or fallback workflows to reduce processing time. Data profiling has a significant impact here, providing a snapshot of your dataset's condition and helping to identify potential issues before they grow.

Data Quality Checklist

- schema validation

- data type checks

- consistency validation

- business rule compliance

- completeness checks

Error Handle Protocol

- retry mechanism defined

- fallback workflows documented

- error logging implemented

- alert thresholds set

Scheduling and Automation of Batch Jobs

Finally, we arrive at the scheduling and automation of batch jobs. Automation is the key to efficiency, reducing manual intervention and freeing up resources for more strategic tasks. Cron jobs, along with more sophisticated schedulers, allow for precise control over execution times, ensuring processes run during optimal periods. Features like dependency tracking and prioritization are useful when managing multiple jobs to prevent bottlenecks. Monitoring should never be overlooked here; investing in alerting for failures allows swift responses to processing hiccups, minimizing downtime, and maintaining data pipeline health. Optimizing execution times further contributes to overall system efficiency, ensuring your resources are used effectively.

Parallelism Strategies

Setting up parallel processing in batch ETL systems needs a balanced resource allocation. Find tasks that run independently—this suit parallelization. Data validation checks across different columns run concurrently, alongside transformations on separate data partitions. Use dynamic partition assignment for even distribution of workloads across available resources.

Resource optimization targets the efficient use of computing power. Set up adaptive resource allocation, where the system dynamically changes the degree of parallelism based on available resources and current workload. Add back pressure mechanisms, reducing downstream bottlenecks when processing speeds vary between stages.

Performance monitoring and tuning in parallel environments needs metrics tracking. Create detailed monitoring of key performance indicators, including processor utilization, memory consumption, and I/O patterns. This monitoring helps identify bottlenecks and optimize resource allocation. Apply predictive scaling based on historical patterns, preparing resources before peak processing periods.

Actionable Optimization Tips for Processing Pipelines

Modern data processing demands speed and performance. Here are practical tips and techniques for optimizing both batch and real-time data processing pipelines.

Performance Tuning Techniques

First up, performance tuning techniques. Improving your queries makes a significant difference. When SQL queries perform well, they drastically reduce execution time. Select only the data you need—use specific column names instead of "*," and apply WHERE clauses to filter records at the source. This reduces the volume of data in your pipeline, reducing time and resources.

Data Filtering: Then, reduce data size through filtering. When a system processes daily sales data, replace all historical sales data with incremental updates that append new entries or modifications. This method increases speed and reduces the load on your infrastructure.

Storage Formats: Storage formats like Parquet or Avro improve throughput. These formats compress data and deliver faster read times compared to standard CSV or JSON files. This creates considerable performance gains in data pipelines.

Data Ingestion: Advanced data ingestion optimization uses intelligent batching strategies. Instead of processing records individually, group them into optimal batch sizes based on your system's characteristics. With streaming data, implement dynamic batch sizing that adjusts based on incoming data velocity—smaller batches during low-traffic periods and larger ones during peak times to maximize throughput and sustain processing efficiency.

Increase throughput with parallel processing. Create multiple ingestion workers to process data simultaneously, each handling a specific partition or segment of the incoming data stream. Add write-ahead logging (WAL) mechanisms for data durability and high ingestion rates. Use memory-mapped files for temporary storage during ingestion, reducing I/O overhead and boosting processing speed.

Resource Allocation and Scaling

Understanding resource allocation and scaling starts with tuning resources based on workload demands. When workloads spike during peak hours, scalable systems allow pipelines to handle increased traffic without lag. Dynamic scaling adjusts the resources allocated to processes based on current demand. This offers flexibility and prevents over-provisioning resources during quiet periods.

Load Balancing

Load balancing is another critical strategy. Distributing incoming data evenly across servers prevents bottlenecks and allows for a smoother flow of information. When implementing efficient load-balancing algorithms, each server handles its fair share of the load, maintaining optimal performance.

Monitoring and Observability

Effective monitoring helps sustain high-performance data pipelines. Track system health through metrics and alerts. Apply monitoring tools to track key performance indicators—like latency, error rates, and throughput—showing how your pipeline performs in real time.

Monitoring Tools: Tools like Prometheus and Grafana are invaluable for logging and visualizing these metrics. They help identify trends or anomalies that might suggest underlying issues. Observability helps teams troubleshoot problems before they escalate, minimizing downtime and keeping things running smoothly.

Alerts: Part of being proactive with your systems involves setting up alerts. This means configuring automated notifications for potential issues—such as when processing time exceeds a certain threshold or when error rates spike. Having this early warning system allows teams to respond swiftly and mitigate problems before users even notice.

Interactive Optimization Process

Finally, there's the iterative optimization process. Setting benchmarks is essential. It acts like a baseline, helping you measure progress as optimizations are applied. Regularly review these benchmarks to ensure that improvements are actually taking effect.

Feedback Loops: Building feedback loops into your process fosters continuous improvement. After making adjustments, monitor the impact on your system. Gather data, analyze results, and make further tweaks as necessary. This cyclical approach keeps your pipelines efficient and adaptable to changing conditions.

Case Studies: Let's look at relevant case studies. For example, companies like Netflix have demonstrated successful optimizations by iteratively improving their systems. Through experimentation and constant refinement, they've achieved impressive scalability and efficiency, handling vast amounts of data seamlessly. These stories serve as inspiration and practical examples of applying iterative optimization in real-world settings.

Final Assessment Exercise

Document your current pipeline

- processing type

- major bottlenecks

- optimization opportunities

Create an optimization plan

- short-term goals

- long-term goals

- resource requirements

Implementation timeline

- Phase 1:

- Phase 2:

- Phase 3:

Key Takeaways

- Success in data processing requires careful selection of appropriate ETL tools and creation of efficient workflows, with tools like Apache NiFi and Talend offering different features suited to specific project needs.

- Effective data pipeline management depends on multiple factors: data quality control, scheduling, resource allocation, and load-balancing—all working together to handle growing datasets.

- System performance can be optimized through various methods, from choosing efficient storage formats to implementing comprehensive monitoring systems.

Chapter 5

Real-World Scaling—How to Handle Growth Without Sacrificing Performance

anaging growth in data systems without sacrificing performance challenges every data engineer and software developer. As applications grow and user loads increase, maintaining optimal performance matters most. Scaling strategies help systems handle more users and data without faltering or slowing down. Both enhancing existing resources and expanding them, understanding these strategies improves application performance in real-world scenarios. Learn the scaling fundamentals with a roadmap for managing growth.

Here, you will

- master vertical and horizontal scaling concepts.

- implement effective load-balancing.

- optimize Redis caching strategies.

- balance performance and cost considerations.

Vertical and Horizontal Scaling Concepts

Data systems need consistent performance when applications expand, and user numbers rise. Two primary methods of scaling are vertical scaling and horizontal scaling, which affect performance and resource management differently. Data engineers and software developers must understand these concepts to build high-performing systems.

Vertical Scaling Explained

Vertical scaling, often referred to as "scaling up," focuses on enhancing the capacity of a single server by adding more powerful components like a faster CPU or additional RAM. This approach can significantly improve performance by allowing a single machine to handle more tasks or process larger datasets.

Limitations: However, it comes with inherent limitations. As you continuously upgrade a server, you eventually hit a ceiling where further enhancements become either impossible due to hardware limits or economically unfeasible. For instance, while adding more RAM might help initially, there will be a point where the costs outweigh the benefits, particularly if the entire system depends on a single point of failure.

Effective Implementation: Vertical scaling proves particularly effective in specific scenarios where application architecture favors centralized processing. For example, in-memory databases like Redis or memory-intensive analytics applications benefit significantly from vertical scaling due to their reliance on single-instance performance. Financial trading systems, where ultra-low latency is crucial, often leverage powerful single servers to minimize network overhead and processing time.

To implement vertical scaling effectively, follow these steps:

- First, establish performance baselines and find resource bottlenecks through comprehensive monitoring.

- Choose component upgrades based on specific needs.

- When database operations max out CPU capacity, upgrade processors before adding memory.

- Add resource-aware application features to dynamically match resource use with hardware capacity.

Optimize performance in vertical scaling by adjusting system settings to get the most from your hardware. This means adjusting operating system parameters, such as kernel settings and I/O schedulers, to match your upgraded hardware. Set up smart caching strategies to use increased memory capacity and apply modern CPU features like advanced vector extensions (AVX) for compute-intensive operations. Split vertical partitioning of databases to maximize increased storage capabilities while maintaining performance.

Vertical scaling brings significant cost considerations. High-performance server upgrades can be expensive and might exceed an organization's budgetary constraints. While vertical scaling works well for applications requiring substantial computing power without distributed architecture complexity, teams should watch when this approach reaches diminishing returns. Technical teams can plan better by knowing when vertical scaling fits their needs, particularly for applications with linear growth patterns requiring fewer constant scaling adjustments.

Resource Upgrade Priority Matrix

Component	Impact	Cost	Implementation Complexity
CPU	High	High	Medium
RAM	High	Medium	Low
Storage	Medium	Low	Low
Network	Medium	Medium	Medium

Horizontal Scaling Explained

Alternatively, horizontal scaling, otherwise known as "scaling out," involves adding more machines or nodes to accommodate increased loads. This strategy brings notable advantages such as redundancy and fault tolerance. When distributing workloads across multiple servers, the system can remain operational even if one node fails, thus enhancing overall reliability. Horizontal scaling supports applications with fluctuating workloads, providing the flexibility to add or remove resources as needed. However, it introduces complexities concerning data consistency and integrity.

Challenges: One key challenge in horizontal scaling is ensuring consistent data across all nodes. Inconsistencies might arise if different servers process data updates at varying times. Addressing this requires solid strategies to maintain data integrity, such as implementing distributed-consistent algorithms that ensure simultaneous data updates across nodes. Another aspect worth considering is network latency, which could impact performance if servers are geographically dispersed. Despite these challenges, the appeal of horizontal scaling lies in its ability to offer virtually unlimited growth potential by continuously integrating new servers.

Workload Distribution: For those seeking practical insights into horizontal scaling, familiarizing yourself with common workload distribution patterns is beneficial. Techniques like sharding or partitioning can optimize database interactions and mitigate latency issues. Sharding involves breaking down large datasets into smaller, manageable segments, allowing parallel processing across numerous servers. Such practices are invaluable for applications experiencing rapid growth or unpredictable spikes in user activity, providing scalability without compromising performance.

Data Consistency Patterns

Pattern	Use Case	Pros	Cons
Strong Consistency	Financial Transactions	Data accuracy	Higher latency
Eventual Consistency	Social media feeds	Better performance	Temporary inconsistency

Casual Consistency	Collaborative apps	Balance of both	Complex implementation

Scaling Comparison Matrix

Aspect	Vertical Scaling	Horizontal Scaling
Definition	Adding power to existing servers	Adding more servers
Cost Model	High upfront costs	Distributed costs over time
Complexity	Lower complexity	Higher complexity
Scalability Limit	Hardware limitations	Theoretically unlimited
Downtime Risk	Higher (single point failure)	Lower (redundancy)
Use Cases	Memory-intensive apps, Analytics	Web apps, Distributed systems

Hybrid Scaling Approaches

Often, the most effective scaling strategy involves a hybrid approach, blending vertical and horizontal scaling elements. Hybrid scaling allows for tailored solutions based on specific application needs, combining the simplicity and power of vertical scaling with the expansiveness and reliability of horizontal scaling. Implementing a hybrid model needs careful planning and consideration of various factors, including anticipated growth patterns, current infrastructure capabilities, and workload characteristics. The balance between the two should enhance performance while minimizing resource wastage and optimizing cost-effectiveness.

Cost Considerations in Scaling

Economic implications play a central role in scaling decisions. Organizations must evaluate the return on investment (ROI) for different scaling strategies to ensure financial viability. This evaluation includes examining upfront costs, ongoing maintenance expenses, and expected performance improvements. Also, predicting future demands is integral to choosing the right scaling strategy; overestimating requirements can lead to excessive spending, whereas underestimating can result in degraded performance and lost opportunities.

Strategic Planning

Balance performance needs and budget limits through strategic planning. Create comprehensive scaling plans focusing on long-term goals instead of immediate wins. Through thorough cost-benefit analyses and careful resource management, technical teams can build scaling solutions matching both operational objectives and fiscal policies.

Integration of Load-Balancing and Caching With Redis

When building data-intensive applications, managing growth without compromising performance presents complex challenges. Start by understanding load-balancing and caching mechanisms, particularly through Redis. These tools power-efficient system scaling—here's what makes them valuable.

Load Balancing Fundamentals

First, let's talk about load-balancing. Imagine your application as a bustling highway during rush hour. Without proper traffic management, you'd have chaos. Load-balancing works like the traffic lights, directing the incoming network traffic across various servers. This prevents any single server from being overwhelmed by a deluge of requests.

Algorithms: Now, how does it achieve this magical feat? Through algorithms like round-robin and least connections. Round-robin is like taking turns evenly—each server in line receives an equal share of the requests. On the other hand, the least connections method is a smart detective—it identifies which server currently handles the fewest connections and directs the new traffic that way. When strategically spreading the load, these techniques increase reliability, especially during unexpected traffic spikes when everyone seems to want a piece of your app simultaneously.

Real-World Examples: Major e-commerce platforms show the power of effective load-balancing in action. Consider an online retailer that implemented a dynamic load-balancing strategy during their annual sale event. Their system successfully handled a 500% increase in traffic by automatically distributing requests across a cluster of application servers. The implementation involved a combination of health checks and predictive scaling, resulting in 99.99% uptime during peak periods.

Another success story comes from a streaming service that deployed geographic load-balancing. Simply by routing users to the nearest server cluster, they reduced latency by 40% and improved video buffering times by 60%. Their implementation included real-time health monitoring and automatic failover mechanisms, ensuring uninterrupted service even when regional servers experienced issues.

Load Balancer Algorithm Comparison

Algorithm	Best For	Limitations
Round Robin	Simple distribution	Doesn't consider server load
Least Connections	Dynamic workload	Additional overhead
IP Hash	Session persistence	Potential uneven distribution
Weighted Round Robin	Mixed server capabilities	Manual weight configuration

Introduction to Redis Caching

Load balancing alone can't solve all problems. This is where Redis provides an in-memory database solution. Traditional databases run slowly, mainly because they store data on disks. Redis changes this pattern by keeping everything in memory, reducing latency in data access. Think of it as a superfast search engine for your commonly accessed data.

Using key-value store concepts, Redis performs rapid data retrieval, supporting systems that need speed.

Cache Management: Redis offers additional features. Redis manages cached data using cache eviction policies. This works like housekeeping. Policies like Least Recently Used (LRU) or Least Frequently Used (LFU) prevent your cache from getting cluttered with unnecessary old data. These policies retain only the most valuable, frequently requested data for optimal performance.

Combining Load-Balancing With Caching

The advantage of combining load balancers with Redis caching comes from their synergy. Moving routine tasks like fetching frequent data from the database to Redis improves system efficiency. Traffic flows smoothly, and response times are lightning-fast. However, putting them together isn't enough; they need proper configuration. Misconfigurations can lead to bottlenecks, eliminating the benefits they offer. Setting the right balance between cache size and eviction policy matters most. An oversized cache can waste resources, while a too-small one fails at storing necessary data.

Architecture Details

The integration of load balancers with Redis requires careful architectural consideration. A typical high-performance setup involves multiple layers: Front-end load balancers distribute incoming traffic, while application servers maintain persistent connections to Redis clusters. Implementation patterns often include:

- Session stickiness configuration to ensure related requests from the same user hit the same application server.

- Redis cluster sharding for optimal data distribution.

- Redundant Redis instances for high availability.

- Write-through and write-behind caching strategies for data consistency.

Configuration strategies should focus on optimizing both components:

- Load balancer health check intervals tuned to application characteristics.

- Connection pooling settings aligned with Redis cluster capacity.

- Timeout configurations that prevent cascade failures.

- Cache TTL values based on data access patterns and freshness requirements.

Redis Configuration Exercise

Configure Redis Caching:

- Cache Strategy

  - cache size

  - eviction policy

  - TTL settings

- Data Access Patterns

  - read/Write ratio

  - hot key identification

  - persistence requirements

- Monitoring Setup

  - key metrics

  - alert Thresholds

  - backup strategy

Best Practices for Implementation

Now, onto the best practices. To truly leverage these technologies, your focus should be on configuring solutions accurately. Start by understanding your traffic patterns. Are there particular times when the load surges? Adjust your load balancer settings to accommodate these peaks dynamically. Regular monitoring is non-negotiable. Keep tabs on server health and identify any anomalies before they spiral out of control.

Resource Management

Also, don't shy away from reallocating resources in real time. This flexibility allows efficiency during surprise traffic jumps. Automate this process wherever possible, leveraging modern tools that adapt based on predefined metrics. Scalability isn't a set-it and forget-it affair; it demands constant attention and tweaking.

Continuous Improvement

Lastly, promote a culture of continuous learning. As technology evolves, so do strategies for optimizing performance. Stay updated with the latest advancements in load-balancing algorithms and Redis features. Engage with communities or forums where professionals share insights and troubleshoot common issues.

Cost Comparison Framework

Component	Vertical Cost	Horizontal Cost
Hardware	High upfront	Distributed
Licensing	Per server	Per node
Maintenance	Centralized	Distributed
Network	Lower	Higher
Operations	Simpler	Complex

Final Integration Exercise

Create a comprehensive scaling strategy

1. Current State Analysis

      a. performance metrics

      b. cost structure

      c. technical debt

2.   Target Architecture

      a. scaling approach

      b. technology stack

      c. implementation phases

3.   Migration Plan

      a. timeline

      b. resource requirements

      c. risk mitigation

Key Takeaways

- Data systems can be scaled through two primary approaches: vertical scaling (upgrading individual servers) and horizontal scaling (distributing across multiple servers), each with distinct advantages and limitations.

- Vertical scaling offers simpler implementation but faces eventual hardware limits and budget constraints, while horizontal scaling provides better reliability and growth potential but introduces complexity in data consistency and network performance.

- A hybrid approach, combining both vertical and horizontal scaling strategies, often provides the most effective solution by leveraging the strengths of each method.

Chapter 6

Mastering Databases for High Throughput

Database optimization maximizes transaction and query performance. This process improves speed and efficiency, especially for large-scale data operations. When milliseconds matter, optimized database performance gives you a competitive advantage. Your applications can handle traffic spikes and process data smoothly when you master optimization techniques.

Here, you will

- understand the key differences between SQL and NoSQL databases.

- learn how to implement high-availability database systems.

- master replication strategies and clustering technologies.

- develop skills in database performance monitoring.

Choosing Between SQL and NoSQL Databases

Selecting the right database type is important for achieving high throughput in data-intensive applications. It hinges significantly on understanding specific use cases and matching them with the appropriate database characteristics. One size does not fit all, especially when it comes to databases. Developers and engineers need to weigh several factors to make an informed decision.

Database Selection Checklist

- Define your data structure requirements.

- Identify transaction consistency needs.

- Evaluate expected read/write ratios.

- Consider scaling requirements.

- Assess development team expertise.

SQL Database Characteristics

Starting with SQL databases, these systems are grounded in relational data models and have long been trusted for their ACID compliance: atomicity, consistency, isolation, and durability. This means they are reliable for transactions; they ensure that all parts of a transaction are completed, or none are, maintaining consistency even in the event of errors or crashes. Such a mechanism makes SQL databases ideal for applications requiring complex queries and stringent data consistency. For instance, financial applications where precise and consistent transaction records are vital heavily rely on SQL databases. Also, the structured nature of SQL databases supports operations like joins, which can be pivotal in drawing meaningful connections between datasets.

SQL Database Strengths	SQL Database Limitations
ACID Compliance	Vertical Scaling Limits
Complex Queries	Schema Rigidity
Data Integrity	Higher Costs at Scale
Join Operations	Complex Sharding

Eventual Consistency Models and Their Performance Implications

Performance optimization in SQL databases needs strategic indexing and thoughtful query design. Well-placed indexes speed up query performance by creating efficient pathways to data retrieval. This optimization has costs; each index increases storage requirements and slows down write operations. Database administrators should weigh these considerations when designing their optimization strategy.

Good queries also improve database performance. Studying query execution plans shows how databases process requests and reveals potential bottlenecks. This insight helps restructure queries efficiently through reordering JOIN operations, refining WHERE clauses, or placing subqueries. Query optimization needs to understand the syntax and how the database engine interprets and executes these commands.

Modern SQL databases include sophisticated monitoring features. These features show query execution paths and resource utilization patterns, supporting data-driven decisions about optimization strategies. Using these methods, organizations can significantly improve their database performance while maintaining data integrity.

NoSQL Database Characteristics

On the flip side, NoSQL databases are designed for flexibility and scalability. They ditch the conventional table-based relational database structure for unstructured or semi-structured forms, which can effortlessly handle large volumes of diverse data types. This makes NoSQL particularly appealing for big data scenarios, allowing horizontal scaling across distributed architectures. Such capabilities are essential for applications dealing with a vast amount of data that need rapid growth potential, such as social media platforms or IoT applications that collect sensor data from numerous devices.

NoSQL Type	Best Used For	Example Use Case
Document	Semi-structured data	Content management
Key-Value	High-speed access	Session management

Column-family	Large-scale analytics	Time-series data
Graph	Connected data	Social networks

Use Case Scenarios

The choice between SQL and NoSQL often boils down to the specific performance requirements dictated by the use case scenarios. For transactional systems where reliability and data integrity are paramount, SQL databases offer robust solutions. Consider online banking systems; here, the capability for efficient multi-row transactions while making sure data precision is indispensable, making SQL the go-to option. Conversely, when the need for quick reads and writes at scale takes precedence, NoSQL databases shine. E-commerce giants, for example, benefit from NoSQL's ability to manage customer interactions in real time, handling sessions, shopping carts, and user recommendations without breaking a sweat.

Data Modeling and Design

While choosing a database type, you should not overlook the importance of data modeling and design, as they substantially affect database performance. In SQL databases, normalization—the process of organizing data to reduce redundancy—is key to optimizing storage efficiency and query speed. However, this can make databases slightly more complex, leading to potentially slower read times. On the other hand, NoSQL databases, given their flexible schemas, often employ denormalization, wherein redundant data storage is acceptable if it improves read performance. This practice can substantially speed up access times, a boon for applications prioritizing fast data retrieval.

Continuous Reevaluation of Data Schema

As applications evolve, the underlying data schemas must adapt to accommodate changing requirements and growing data volumes. This evolution presents challenges and opportunities for database administrators and developers. Regular schema evaluation becomes essential as applications scale, and user needs change. This ongoing process makes sure that the database structure continues to serve the application's needs efficiently while maintaining optimal performance.

Schematic evolution in production environments needs careful planning and execution. Changes must be implemented in ways that minimize disruption to existing operations while ensuring data integrity throughout the transition process. This might involve phased approaches to schema updates, careful monitoring of system performance during transitions, and maintaining backward compatibility where necessary.

Decision Guidelines

To aid in deciding between SQL and NoSQL, here's a guideline:

- Begin by analyzing your application's requirements.

- Identify if the priority is on strong transaction support and data consistency or if the need is for handling large-scale, dynamic data sets with ease.

- If your application leans toward frequent updates and complex querying and requires strict adherence to ACID properties, SQL might be your best bet.

- If you're expecting to scale massively, need schema flexibility, and require speedy performance in extracting insights from potentially terabytes of data, NoSQL could serve your needs better.

Future Considerations

Reflect on the potential future growth of your application. Understanding whether your data workload will remain steady or skyrocket can influence the database decision. Planning for scalability from the beginning can save considerable headaches down the line. Remember, transitioning from SQL to NoSQL at a later stage, or vice versa, involves significant time and resource investments.

Implementing High-Availability Database Systems

When you're setting up a highly available database system, the idea is to ensure it's always ready and running, even during hiccups.

Replication Strategies

One of the main tricks up your sleeve is replication strategies. Imagine you've got a master-slave setup, where you have one primary database handling all the write operations and one or more replicas (or slaves) taking care of read requests. This configuration helps balance the load and keeps things moving smoothly, even if the primary decides to hit the snooze button. Multi-master setups can also be handy, especially if you want every database node to both read and write data, creating a more flexible and resilient system. With either approach, automatic failover is important. You don't want to be scrambling to fix issues manually every time something goes wrong. Automatic failover means that if one node in your database goes offline, another picks up the slack without missing a beat.

Database replication maintains continuity. Database outages during peak hours can stop business operations. Primary-replica setups keep backup databases ready for immediate failover. In contrast, distributed systems use active-active deployment, where different nodes handle different operations simultaneously. Each node processes tasks independently yet cooperatively. Select the setup based on your operational needs, including read-heavy versus write-heavy loads, geographic distribution, and maintenance.

Selecting Appropriate Replication Factors Based on Application Needs

Choosing the right replication factor maintains optimal data availability while managing system resources. This number—how many data copies exist across nodes—depends on several key considerations. Systems with sensitive data need a higher replication factor for better redundancy and fault tolerance. This increases storage costs and makes data consistency harder to maintain.

When determining your replication factor, consider your application's specific requirements for data durability, read performance, and geographic distribution. For instance, applications serving users across multiple regions might benefit from a higher replication factor with strategically placed replicas to reduce latency. On the other hand, applications with less stringent availability requirements might operate efficiently with fewer replicas, reducing operational overhead and complexity.

Clustering Technologies

Understanding clustering technologies helps in distributing load. With clusters, databases distribute user requests across several instances. Beyond failover protection, clustering improves performance by sharing workload.

In clustering, two main approaches exist:

Shared-nothing clusters separate all resources—they operate independently; this reduces bottlenecks but requires data partitioning strategies.

Shared-disk allows all nodes to access common storage, simplifying data coherence but requiring concurrency controls.

Choosing the right clustering strategy can dramatically impact your system's resilience and scalability. Shared-nothing is often preferred for its ability to scale horizontally and avoid single points of failure. Yet, it requires thoughtful data partitioning and consistency models. On the other hand, shared-disk architecture might seem simpler to manage, but you need efficient mechanisms to handle concurrent access to the same data. A practical guideline would be to assess your specific workload and scalability requirements, choosing a strategy that minimizes latency and maximizes availability.

Clustering Decision Matrix

Factor	Shared-Nothing	Shared-Disk
Scalability	Horizontal	Vertical
Data Consistency	Complex	Simpler
Resource Usage	Independent	Shared
Maintenance	Per Node	Centralized

Cluster Monitoring Tools and Alerts for Nodes Failures

Implementing solid monitoring systems for cluster health is absolutely essential for maintaining optimal database performance. Specialized monitoring tools can track individual node status, network connectivity, and resource utilization across the cluster. These tools should be configured to provide immediate alerts when nodes show signs of deterioration or failure, enabling proactive intervention before issues affect system availability.

Key metrics to monitor include

- node response times

- resource utilization patterns

- inter-node communication latency.

Setting up automated alerts for these metrics helps identify potential issues early. For example, if a node consistently shows higher latency or unusual resource consumption patterns, the monitoring system can trigger alerts, allowing administrators to investigate and address the root cause before it leads to node failure. Regular analysis of these monitoring metrics also helps in capacity planning and optimization of cluster resources.

Failover Mechanisms

Failover mechanisms are the safety nets of your database operations. The goal is for the transition from an active node to a standby one to be seamless, requiring minimal human intervention. Efficient failover protocols mean less downtime and quicker recovery. Implementing automated failover solutions demands careful orchestration to maintain data integrity and consistency. Without the proper setup, you risk data loss or corruption when switches occur. It's essential to test failover processes regularly in a controlled environment to iron out any kinks before they can cause real issues.

Failover strategies come in various flavors; some involve pre-configured standby servers that spring into action when needed, while others rely on dynamic allocation based on current demand. An effective guideline would be to regularly simulate failovers, ensuring your system responds correctly and maintains data integrity throughout the process.

Consistency checks and thorough testing processes are indispensable for a reliable failover mechanism.

Performance Monitoring Tools

Performance monitoring tools are like your personal watchdogs, keeping an eye on database health and alerting you when something seems off. These tools track everything from server load to query performance, providing insights into potential bottlenecks before they escalate into problems. Real-time alerts are critical—imagine getting a notification about a problematic query before it slows down your entire system. With advanced performance analysis, you can tweak and fine-tune your database settings proactively instead of constantly playing catch-up with issues.

Through performance monitoring, teams can predict and fix potential failures. Regular database maintenance creates a smoother user experience and prevents unexpected downtimes. Tracking metrics and adjusting configurations maintains your database performance to handle increased loads.

Key Takeaways

- Database selection between SQL and NoSQL should be based on specific use cases: SQL excels at reliability and data integrity, while NoSQL offers better performance for high-volume, speed-critical applications.

- System availability and reliability depend on implementing proper high-availability configurations and effective replication strategies (whether primary-replica or distributed setups).

- Clustering helps prevent performance bottlenecks by distributing database workloads across multiple nodes.

Chapter 7

Real-Time Applications—How to Build Low-Latency Systems

Low-latency systems power modern applications, where real-time applications need prompt data processing and delivery. From powering a live chat application, streaming sports scores, or updating financial stock tickers, quick data flow creates smooth and immediate user experiences. In our chapter on "Real-Time Applications," we explore strategies and techniques needed for building such efficient systems. We present various methodologies for swift and seamless data handling, meeting users' needs for instant responses. This exploration of low-latency solutions shows how adjustments and informed choices can improve your application's performance, reducing lag and increasing user satisfaction.

Here, you will

- master WebSocket implementation for real-time messaging.

- optimize performance with in-memory databases.

- implement effective caching strategies.

- secure real-time communications.

Building Real-Time Messaging Systems With WebSockets

WebSockets are an incredible tool for creating low-latency communication channels essential for real-time messaging applications. Essentially, WebSockets allow for a two-way connection over a single TCP link, providing a persistent and interactive way to exchange data in real time. Unlike the traditional HTTP protocol, where connections are short-lived and request-response-based, WebSockets maintain open connections, facilitating instant communication between client and server.

Consider how typical HTTP connections operate—each interaction follows a strict pattern: request, response, then termination. This cycle, while effective for retrieving static web pages, becomes cumbersome when you need continuous data flow, such as in live chatting or notifications. Here's where WebSockets shine. Once established, a WebSocket connection remains open, allowing messages to flow in both directions without the delays inherent in HTTP handshakes. This persistence minimizes latency sharply, making applications feel swift and responsive.

Imagine using a chat application underpinned by WebSockets. Messages you type appear instantly on your friend's screen, enabling a seamless, dynamic conversation. In scenarios like stock market tickers or sports scores where timely updates are crucial, WebSockets ensure the data reaches users without lag, maintaining engagement and satisfaction.

Implementing WebSockets in Node.js

Transitioning a system to use WebSockets has several steps, especially when working within a Node.js environment. Node.js, known for its event-driven architecture, makes implementing WebSockets relatively straightforward, thanks to libraries like Socket.IO, which abstract many complexities. When setting this up, it's important to initialize the server to handle WebSocket events and establish client-side scripting that communicates effectively with the server.

Error Handling, Connection Management, and Code Organization Best Practices

Developers must handle errors while working with WebSocket connections. Strong error management maintains system stability and creates a better user experience. This includes managing connection drops, timeout scenarios, and message delivery failures. Implement automatic reconnection logic, message queuing for failed deliveries, and clear error messaging to clients.

Connection management becomes particularly important as your application scales. Implementing connection pooling, heartbeat mechanisms to detect stale connections, and graceful connection termination protocols helps maintain system reliability. For instance, implementing a ping-pong mechanism ensures connections remain active and allows quick detection of disconnected clients.

When organizing WebSocket code, following a modular approach improves maintainability and scalability. Separating connection handling, message processing, and business logic into distinct modules makes the codebase easier to maintain and test. Consider implementing event-driven patterns that cleanly separate concerns:

- Connection management layer for handling client connections.

- Message processing layer for handling different types of messages.

- Business logic layer for implementing specific application features.

Protocol Comparison Matrix

Feature	WebSocket	HTTP/REST	Long Polling
Connection Type	Persistent	Temporary	Intermittent
Overhead	Low	High	Medium
Real-Time Capability	Native	Limited	Simulated
Server Push	Yes	No	Limited
Implementation Complexity	Medium	Low	High

Scalability	Complex	Simple	Moderate

Exercise WebSocket Connection Analysis

Analyze your application's needs:

1. Current Communication Pattern

    a. request frequency (per second):

    b. message size (KB):

    c. bidirectional needs: Yes/No

    d. latency requirements (ms):

2. Expected Scale

    a. concurrent users:

    b. message throughput (msg/sec):

    c. peak load periods:

3. Calculate Resource Requirements

    a. memory per connection (KB):

    b. total memory needed (GB):

    c. network bandwidth (Mbps):

Security Considerations

However, what's efficiency without security? This is where the significance of using secure WebSocket connections (wss://) comes into play. Just as securing regular web traffic with *https* is relevant, securing WebSocket connections prevents unauthorized interceptions, allowing user data to remain confidential. Setting up these secure connections isn't difficult but requires attention to detail, like acquiring SSL certificates and configuring them correctly on the server.

Beyond the encryption layer, safeguarding payload integrity through user validation is critical. Making sure only authenticated users can access sensitive data or perform certain operations adds an important security boundary. Methods such as token-based authentication can be integrated to verify users before initiating a WebSocket connection. It's also wise to validate data at the application level, checking message formats and content to prevent potential misuse or attacks like injection or flooding.

Following these security practices protects the system from threats and builds confidence in users, as their interactions remain protected. Regular updates and security fixes for WebSocket implementations guard against newly discovered vulnerabilities and defend against new threats.

Security Checklist Template

WebSocket Security Configuration

- Connection Security

    o SSL/TLS implementation

    o certificate validation

    o protocol enforcement (wss://)

- Authentication

    o token-based auth setup

    o session management

    o connection validation

- Message Security

    o payload encryption

- ○ data validation

- ○ rate limiting

Security Risk Assessment Matrix

Risk	Impact	Likelihood	Mitigation
Man-in-middle	High	Medium	TLS, Payload encryption
DDos	High	Medium	Rate limiting, Connection pools
Data injection	High	High	Input validation, Sanitization
Authentication bypass	Critical	Low	Token verification, Session management

Use Cases of WebSockets

The adoption of WebSockets doesn't just hinge on technical benefits; it also transforms the end-user experience. When reducing latency and offering a more cohesive data flow, WebSockets empower real-time applications to deliver consistent and reliable user experiences. Whether for social platforms, collaborative tools, or notification systems, leveraging WebSocket technology provides the backbone needed for rapid and flexible communication.

Case Studies and Scaling Challenges

Real-world implementations of WebSockets show their versatility and power. Take collaborative document editing platforms, where multiple users can simultaneously edit a document and see changes in real time. These systems handle complex scenarios like conflict resolution and cursor position synchronization while maintaining low latency across numerous concurrent connections.

Scaling real-time applications presents certain challenges that WebSockets help address. As user numbers grow, considerations like connection limits, memory usage, and server capacity become very important. Implementing clustering and load-balancing strategies helps distribute the connection load across multiple servers. Some common challenges include

- Managing connection state across multiple server instances.

- Handling broadcast messages efficiently to thousands of connected clients.

- Maintaining consistent message ordering in distributed systems.

- Implementing rate limiting to prevent system overload.

Reducing Latency With In-Memory Databases and Smart Caching

Alright, real-time applications demand lightning-fast data retrieval and processing to function effectively. This is where leveraging in-memory databases and caching strategies is really important. When we consider scenarios like gaming leaderboards, the need for quick data access becomes glaringly evident. Say a player overtakes another on the leaderboard, and this change is not being updated instantly; it would surely hamper the user experience. When storing data directly in RAM rather than on a disk, in-memory databases provide significant performance advantages because RAM allows much faster access times compared to traditional storage methods.

Implementing in-memory databases is especially beneficial when high-demand situations need rapid response times. A simple illustration outside of gaming might be stock trading applications, where every millisecond can be critical. Here, latency must be minimized to offer users the most current data instantly, ensuring their decisions are based on the latest available information.

Database Design and Data Modeling for Optimal Performance

Smart database design and data modeling maximize the benefits of in-memory databases. Create your data schema based on the access patterns of in-memory operations. Consider denormalizing data in in-memory databases since the space trade-off matters less than in disk-based systems, and fewer joins significantly boost performance.

Key considerations for optimal data modeling include:

- Structuring data to minimize memory fragmentation.

- Designing indexes that complement in-memory access patterns.

- Implementing efficient partitioning strategies for large datasets.

- Organizing data to take advantage of memory locality.

Memory management becomes particularly relevant in in-memory databases. Implementing smart memory allocation strategies and garbage collection policies helps maintain consistent performance even under heavy loads.

Database Comparison Table

Feature	Redis	Memcached	Aerospike
Data Types	Multiple	Key-value	Multiple
Persistence	Optional	No	Yes
Clustering	Yes	No	Yes
Memory Efficiency	High	Very high	High
Learning Curve	Medium	Low	High

Introduction to Caching

Let's examine caching mechanisms like Redis and Memcached. These tools dramatically reduce data access time. They temporarily hold frequently accessed data closer to the client, speeding up data access. When you visit an e-commerce site, caching loads product details quickly instead of querying the database on every page load.

Cache Invalidation Strategies

Cache invalidation is one of the two hard problems in computer science (along with naming things and off-by-one errors). Implementing effective cache invalidation strategies is vital for maintaining data consistency without compromising performance. Consider time-based invalidation for relatively static data, and implement event-driven invalidation for frequently updated content.

Key invalidation strategies include:

- Write-through caching, where updates are written to both the cache and database simultaneously.

- Write-behind caching, where updates are initially written to cache and later synchronized with the database.

- Cache-aside patterns are where the application manages the interaction between the cache and the database.

- Implementing versioning to handle concurrent updates and prevent stale data issues.

Practical Exercise: Cache Design

Design your caching strategy:

- data access patterns

- read/write ratio:

- hot data size (GB):

- access frequency (requests/sec):

- data lifetime (hours):

Cache Configuration

- cache size (GB):

- eviction policy:

- TTL settings:

- backup strategy:

Monitoring Plan

- hit rate target (%):

- miss rate threshold (%):

- latency target (ms):

Combining Caching With Real-Time Processing

This means less waiting around and more seamless browsing—an essential feature for maintaining user engagement. Integrating such caching solutions doesn't just focus on raw speed but also greatly enhances user experience during peak loads. Think about live-streaming services during a major sporting event. Implementing caching ensures minimal buffering and smooth playback, even as thousands or millions of users login simultaneously. With caching, you're essentially preemptively loading popular content, so users have immediate access without delay.

Something to remember here is how to effectively introduce caching into your systems.

- Begin by identifying the data that gets requested frequently but doesn't change often, as this represents prime caching material.

- From there, choose a suitable caching mechanism, like Redis, for its ability to handle massive amounts of keys and values efficiently.

- Next, configure the cache settings with optimal expiration policies to balance freshness and resource utilization.

Lazy Loading and Prefetching Techniques

Lazy loading and prefetching techniques can significantly improve cache performance in real-time systems. Lazy loading defers data loading until it's actually needed, reducing initial load times and memory usage. On the flip side, prefetching anticipates future data needs and loads data proactively.

Implementing these techniques requires:

- Analyzing user behavior patterns to predict data access.

- Setting up intelligent prefetching triggers based on user actions.

- Balancing memory usage between lazy-loaded and prefetched data.

- Implementing smart eviction policies for prefetched data that isn't used.

Performance Monitoring and Optimization

Of course, no system is complete without monitoring and optimization. Relying solely on the initial setup won't guarantee sustained performance levels. Monitoring cache performance becomes indispensable. You'll want to track hit ratios, which tell you how often requested data gets served from the cache versus having to pull from the primary database. A high cache hit ratio means your caching strategy is effective, minimizing unnecessary database queries and thus speeding up data access.

Several tools help measure and optimize cache performance. Start by examining your cache's eviction policy. Review how it manages data with low access rates. Configuring these parameters creates a balance between fresh data and fast-read performance. Monitoring these metrics improves performance, keeping your system at peak real-time responsiveness.

Final Integration Challenge

Build a mini real-time system:

Choose Components

- WebSocket library:

- in-memory database:

- caching solution:

Define Architecture

- component diagram: [Draw here]

- data flow: [Describe here]

- security measures: [List here]

Implementation Plan

- timeline:

- resource needs:

- success criteria:

Key Takeaway

- WebSockets provide essential real-time messaging capabilities through persistent connections, making them ideal for applications requiring immediate data updates like chat systems and live sports scores.

- Implementation of WebSockets, particularly with Node.js, requires careful attention to security through encrypted connections and proper user validation protocols.

- In-memory databases and strategic caching systems (using tools like Redis and Memcached) play crucial roles in reducing latency by storing frequently accessed data closer to users.

Chapter 8

Fast Algorithms for Big Data

Processing big data demands speed and efficiency with massive amounts of information—effective algorithms process this data. These algorithms help us process varying data volumes efficiently. Fast algorithms power modern data systems, making complex operations more manageable. They convert immense datasets into valuable insights by streamlining processing. Beyond algorithms, these solutions integrate with distributed computing frameworks. This chapter explains the components that enable efficient data processing.

Here, you will

- master MapReduce implementation with Spark.

- optimize parallel processing techniques.

- implement effective data partitioning.

- configure and tune Spark jobs.

Setting up Distributed MapReduce Jobs With Spark

As we explore big data, efficiently handling vast datasets matters. One programming model that emerges is MapReduce. This framework processes large-scale data across distributed systems. MapReduce excels at parallelizing tasks, letting significant data chunks run simultaneously. It fits perfectly with modern data-intensive applications. Through its mapping and reducing functions, this model helps developers run complex operations on datasets, extracting meaningful insights while using the distributed nature of modern computing environments.

Common MapReduce Use Cases

During implementation, MapReduce applications shows these strengths. Log file analysis becomes a key use case, where server logs reveal user behavior patterns and system performance. Text processing applications, such as word count and document analysis, highlight MapReduce's effectiveness with unstructured data. Graph processing applications, particularly in social network analysis, use MapReduce to map complex relationships and connections. Data aggregation tasks, like analyzing customer purchase patterns across multiple regions, work well with MapReduce's distributed processing capabilities.

Framework Comparison Matrix

Feature	Apache Spark	Hadoop MapReduce	Apache Flink
Processing Type	In-memory	Disk-based	Stream-first
Learning Curve	Moderate	Steep	Moderate
Performance	Fast	Slower	Very Fast
Memory Usage	High	Low	Moderate
Use Cases	Batch & Stream	Batch	Stream & Batch
Community Support	Extensive	Mature	Growing

Practical Implementation Examples

MapReduce's versatility shines in real-world scenarios. For instance, when processing web server logs, MapReduce can simultaneously analyze multiple log files, with the Map function extracting relevant fields and the Reduce function aggregating metrics like user session duration. In e-commerce applications, MapReduce efficiently processes customer transaction data across different geographical regions, enabling real-time inventory management and sales analysis.

Setting up Spark Environment

MapReduce remains daunting to configure and implement. This is why Apache Spark shines. Spark streamlines MapReduce jobs through a unified engine supporting both batch processing and real-time analytics. To use Spark, setting up your environment becomes your first step. Spark's compatibility with various operating systems simplifies setup, though methods differ across your platform.

Windows users set up Spark by downloading the pre-built package from the official website, which lists instructions for configuring system paths. Linux and macOS users can access Spark through package managers or downloadable archives. Each operating system needs different steps; Linux needs to adjust user permissions and verify Java and Scala installations, as these languages support Spark's functionality. All platforms need Java Development Kit (JDK), since Spark runs on top of Java Virtual Machine (JVM). Installing a compatible version of JDK prevents runtime issues later on.

Exercise: Environment Setup

Configure your Spark environment:

System Requirements

- OS:

- Java Version:

- Memory Available (GB):

- Cores Available:

Installation Steps

- Download Spark

- Set JAVA_HOME

- Set SPARK_HOME

- Configure environment variables

- Test installation

Validation Checklist

- spark-shell launches

- sample job runs

- web UI accessible

Understanding Key Spark Components

At the heart of Spark's architecture lies SparkContext, serving as the primary entry point for all Spark functionality. It handles essential tasks like configuration management and cluster connectivity. The modern SparkSession provides an enhanced interface for working with DataFrames and SQL operations, offering a more intuitive approach to data manipulation. Understanding these components is crucial for effective Spark development.

Common Setup Issues and Solutions

In Spark setup, developers face common challenges. JVM heap space configuration should be adjusted to prevent memory-related issues. Conflicts among different Spark components need resolution for smooth operation. Network configuration, particularly in distributed environments, needs proper setup for optimal node communication. Resource allocation works best when optimized for the available hardware and workload demands.

Writing MapReduce Jobs in Spark

With Spark installed, the next challenge is implementing the Map and Reduce functions. Spark provides two robust APIs for this: Resilient Distributed Datasets (RDDs) and

DataFrames. RDDs offer more control over data processing and transformations, appealing to those who require granular manipulation of their data. Meanwhile, DataFrames provide a higher-level abstraction, akin to operating on relational tables in SQL, making them accessible for analysts and developers familiar with database operations.

As you code MapReduce jobs in Spark, understanding data shuffling improves performance. Shuffling moves data across different partitions and nodes during processing, which takes both time and resources. Well-designed maps and reduced functions minimize unnecessary data shuffling, reducing execution times. Using narrow dependencies over wide dependencies between stages limits shuffle operations, improving job efficiency.

MapReduce Use Cases Matrix

Use Case	Input Data	Map Function	Reduce Function	Output
Word Count	Text files	Split into words	Sum counts	Word frequencies
Log Analysis	Server logs	Extract events	Aggregate metrics	Analysis report
Graph Processing	Edge lists	Node mapping	Path reduction	Processed graph
Data ETL	Raw data	Transform	Aggregate	Clean dataset

Code Structure Guidelines

Writing maintainable Spark code requires following established best practices. This includes organizing data input and output operations logically, implementing comprehensive error handling and logging mechanisms, using descriptive variable names that reflect their purpose, and breaking complex transformations into manageable steps. These practices allow code readability and maintainability while facilitating collaborative development.

Code Structure Template

Project Organization

- Data Input Layer

    - source validation

    - schema definition

    - input partitioning

- Processing Layer

    - map functions

    - reduce functions

    - transformation logic

- Output Layer

    - result formatting

    - data persistence

    - error handling

Submitting Jobs to a Cluster

Once your MapReduce job is ready, it's time to submit it to the cluster for execution. Submitting Spark jobs can be carried out through Spark's built-in command-line interface or programmatically via libraries such as Livy that interact with Spark clusters. Using the command-line interface, you specify the master URL of the Spark cluster, along with any additional configuration settings that might be needed based on your specific requirements.

Monitoring these jobs is equally important to know they're running as expected. Spark offers a web UI, accessible at port 4040, which provides a visual overview of active jobs, displaying key metrics like task duration, shuffle read/write times, and resource utilization. This interface is invaluable for identifying potential bottlenecks and optimizing future executions.

Cluster Resource Management

Effective cluster management involves understanding different resource managers like YARN, standalone cluster management, and Mesos integration. Each option offers benefits and requires specific configuration approaches. Dynamic resource allocation enables efficient use of cluster resources by adjusting resource usage based on workload demands.

Advanced Job Monitoring

Beyond basic monitoring, advanced performance analysis involves tracking detailed metrics, optimizing memory usage patterns, detecting data skew issues, and identifying processing bottlenecks. These insights allow proactive optimization and ensure efficient resource utilization across the cluster.

Optimizing Algorithms Through Parallel Processing and Partitioning

Understanding optimizing algorithms for big data through parallel processing and data partitioning helps process data faster. Processing large datasets, speed matters, and parallelism provides a clear solution. Parallelism splits tasks into smaller units running concurrently. Rather than handling one task, multiple processors complete numerous tasks simultaneously. In big data environments with immense data volumes, processors extract insights quickly.

Parallel processing doesn't just rely on having multiple processors; it capitalizes on dividing tasks logically. This division allows systems to manage subsets of data independently and merge results later. In distributed computing, this aspect becomes even more significant as nodes across networks can work collaboratively. The application of these principles ensures systems optimize their resources effectively, leading to quicker data processing times and enhanced overall efficiency.

Data Locality and Performance Impact

Data locality improves parallel processing performance. Keeping data and processing co-located, systems skip unnecessary network transfers and lower latency. Within distributed environments, data movement slows processing times. Applying data locality creates substantial performance improvements for data-intensive applications.

Sequential vs. Parallel Processing Experiments

Experimental results consistently show the advantages of parallel processing over sequential approaches. For instance, when processing large datasets, parallel execution can achieve near-linear speedup with proper resource allocation. Real-world experiments shows how tasks that take hours in sequential processing can be reduced to minutes through effective parallelization. These comparisons provide concrete evidence of the benefits of parallel processing in big data scenarios.

Partitioning Method Comparison

Method	Pros	Cons	Best For	Implementation Complexity
Hash	Even distribution	No data locality	Random access	Low
Range	Data locality	Potential skew	Ordered data	Medium
Round-Robin	Simple Balance	No data relationship	Equal-size partitions	Low
Custom	Optimized for needs	Complex maintenance	Specific requirements	High

Data Partitioning Strategies

To maximize parallel processing, you must understand data partitioning strategies. Data partitioning splits large datasets into manageable segments that can be processed independently. This method improves performance in distributed environments, creating better load-balancing across different nodes and reducing the chances of bottlenecks. Different partitioning techniques include hash partitioning, range partitioning, and round-robin distribution, providing unique benefits.

Hash partitioning disperses data based on hash functions, ensuring even distribution across partitions. Range partitioning divides data into specific ranges, which is ideal for situations where data is naturally segmented by values. Round-robin allocation, while simpler, distributes data evenly without considering content. The choice of partitioning method affects system performance and is often tailored to the specific requirements of an application or dataset.

Implementing Effective Partitioning in Spark

Practical implementation of partitioning in Spark requires careful consideration of data characteristics and processing requirements. The appropriate number of partitions depends on factors like cluster size, data volume, and processing complexity. Common implementation patterns include repartitioning data before expensive operations and coalescing partitions when data volume reduces.

Impact of Incorrect Partitioning

Poor partitioning choices can lead to significant performance degradation. Data skew, where certain partitions contain disproportionate amounts of data, can create processing bottlenecks. Insufficient partitioning can underutilize cluster resources, while excessive partitioning can create unnecessary overhead. Understanding these impacts helps in making informed partitioning decisions.

Optimizing Spark Jobs

When it comes to implementing these concepts using platforms like Apache Spark, there's much to gain from fine-tuning jobs to achieve optimal performance. Spark is a powerful tool in the big data space, allowing rapid data processing through its resilient distributed datasets (RDDs) and dataframes. However, the magic truly happens when tuning Spark jobs. Fine-tuning involves adjusting configurations to improve execution speed and resource utilization.

A common strategy for optimization adjusts the number of executor cores and memory allocations. Adjusting these parameters improves Spark processing of available hardware resources. Proper parallelism levels keep tasks balanced between optimal counts, which stops resource exhaustion or underutilization.

Another noteworthy approach is utilizing broadcast variables and accumulators. Broadcast variables distribute read-only data efficiently, minimizing redundant data copies, while accumulators help aggregate information across executors without excessive data movement. Both of these tools improve performance by reducing communication overhead between nodes, allowing for faster processing.

Resource Configuration Matrix

Resource	Default	Recommended Range	Impact
Executor Cores	1	2–5	Parallelism
Executor Memory	1G	4G–8G	Processing capacity
Partition Size	128MB	128MB–1GB	I/O efficiency
Driver Memory	1G	2G–4G	Coordination capacity

Benchmarking and Profiling Spark Applications

After Spark jobs start running, measuring performance reveals areas for improvement. Benchmarking and profiling work as primary methods to track performance. Benchmarking measures job performance against standard metrics or previous iterations. This shows improvements and highlights inefficiencies. Profiling analyzes the job's execution, finding potential bottlenecks.

To ease this evaluation process, Spark provides tools like Spark UI and monitoring APIs. Spark UI offers insights into the job stages, task execution times, and storage usage, making it simpler to pinpoint problem areas. For a reactive approach, configuring monitoring tools that trigger alerts when specific thresholds are crossed ensures timely interventions. These methods collectively assist in refining job execution, leading to enhanced performance.

These techniques improve the algorithm's efficiency and create scalable and reliable data processing solutions. Success depends on striking the right balance between resources, configurations, and data characteristics for optimal results.

Debug Exercise

Identify Problem

- symptoms

- error messages

- affected stages

Analysis

- resource usage

- data skew check

- network issues

- configuration review

Resolution Plan

- immediate actions

- long-term fixes

- prevention measures

Key Takeaway

- The chapter covered fundamental big data processing concepts, focusing on distributed MapReduce implementation through Apache Spark, including parallel processing and data partitioning strategies.

- Choosing between RDDs and DataFrames requires careful consideration of data control requirements while minimizing data shuffling is crucial for optimizing MapReduce job performance.

- Understanding and implementing proper resource allocation (executor cores and memory) plays a vital role in maximizing system efficiency.

Chapter 9

Building Scalable Microservices—Hands-On With Real-World Architectures

Creating scalable microservices builds systems that can handle growth efficiently. Microservices changed software development, introducing new ways of developing flexible, powerful applications. Microservices focus on designing architectures that resist failures through their modular nature. Breaking applications into smaller, independent services supports fault tolerance, so when one part of the system fails, the rest continue running. This chapter explains how these resilient systems work, replacing bulky monolithic designs with sleek, agile microservices.

Here, you will

- master microservices architecture principles.

- implement fault tolerance and modularity.

- configure Kubernetes for service discovery.

- design effective auto-scaling strategies.

Microservices Benefits: Fault Tolerance and Modularity

Microservices have become a popular approach in the software development world, and for good reason. They fundamentally reshape how systems are built and operated, promoting resilience and modularity in ways that traditional monolithic architectures struggle to match. Let's get into how exactly microservices enhance system resilience and enable modularity.

Imagine your application is like a set of interconnected blocks where each block represents a specific service. In a monolith, if one block fails, it might bring down the whole stack. However, with microservices, only the problematic block faces disruption. This isolation of failures allows the rest of the application to continue functioning smoothly even if an individual service encounters issues. If the payment processing service goes offline due to a bug, other services like account management or order tracking remain unaffected, maintaining overall user experience stability.

The architecture also promotes redundancy through techniques like circuit breakers and fallback strategies. Circuit breakers act as safety switches that prevent a failing service from overloading the system by cutting off requests once a certain threshold is reached. This strategy not only minimizes the risk of cascading failures but also gives the struggling service time to recover. Additionally, fallback strategies provide alternative solutions when a service fails, ensuring that critical services remain operational. If an inventory check fails during peak sale hours, a temporary "out of stock" message can be shown instead of crashing the entire purchase process.

Architecture Comparison Matrix

Aspect	Monolithic	Microservices
Deployment	Single Unit	Independent services
Scaling	Entire application	Individual components
Development	Large teams	Small, focused teams

Technology Stack	Uniform	Flexible per service
Failure Impact	System-wide	Isolated
Release Cycle	Slow, coordinated	Fast, independent

Exercise: Architecture Assessment

Evaluate your application

- Current Architecture

    - system components

    - dependencies

    - deployment frequency

    - team structure

- Microservices Potential

    - candidate services:

    - breaking points:

    - data boundaries:

- Migration Strategy

    - priority services:

    - timeline:

    - risk assessment:

Modularity and Independent Deployment

Microservices give development teams independence to develop, deploy, and update their own service without coordinating with others. This autonomy speeds up deployment and simplifies management tasks. Developers work on updates or new features for each service and deploy them independently. Creating faster iteration cycles at a granular level makes the software adaptable to changing business needs.

Moreover, this model supports continuous integration and continuous deployment (CI/CD) practices. With independent deployment capabilities, CI/CD pipelines can be tailored to individual services, improving efficiency and reducing the risk of one team's updates disrupting another's progress. Service boundaries are clear, which simplifies understanding and debugging, as each service has a focused responsibility and can be managed separately from the others.

Scalability Advantages

Microservices' modularity goes beyond deployment. This includes resource management, too. Every microservice works scaled based on its unique requirements. This fine granularity in scaling creates efficient handling of computing resources, optimizing both performance and cost. During a seasonal sale, increasing the checkout service while keeping ancillary services at regular operation levels maintains responsiveness where it's most needed. This targeted scaling improves customer satisfaction by reducing wait times and cuts unnecessary expenses that might arise from indiscriminately scaling the entire system.

Implementing circuit breakers in a microservices setup does require some guidelines to make sure they're effective. A well-configured circuit breaker should define clear thresholds for request failure rates and response times beyond which the breaker trips. Regularly reviewing these parameters based on real-world data helps maintain optimal performance, as does integrating monitoring tools to alert teams when a circuit breaker is activated.

Circuit Breaker Configuration Template

Circuit Breaker Setup:

Failure Threshold

- error rate (%):

- timeout (ms):

- reset time (s):

Fallback Strategy

- default response:

- cache policy:

- recovery action:

Monitoring

- health metrics:

- alert conditions:

- recovery tracking:

Technology Integration Benefits

Microservices architecture allows teams to introduce new technologies or approaches for specific services without affecting the entire application. This flexibility allows for gradual modernization and optimization of individual components. Teams can experiment with different technologies, frameworks, or databases that best suit their service's specific needs, fostering innovation while maintaining system stability.

Enhanced Collaboration

The microservices approach naturally promotes the formation of smaller, focused teams that take complete ownership of specific services. This ownership leads to increased productivity as teams become deeply familiar with their services' requirements and characteristics. Teams can make decisions quickly and implement changes effectively within their domain of expertise.

Cross-Functional Collaboration

Microservices architecture strengthens cross-functional collaboration by removing traditional development silos. Teams consisting of developers, operations specialists, and business analysts work together on specific services. This collaboration aligns technical decisions with business objectives while services achieve peak performance and functionality.

Innovation and Experimentation

The modular nature of microservices creates a safe environment for experimentation. Teams can innovate on smaller, less critical parts of the system without risking the stability of the entire application. This approach allows rapid prototyping and testing of new features or improvements, accelerating the pace of innovation while maintaining system reliability.

As you can see, microservices create a paradigm shift towards more resilient, flexible, and scalable applications, addressing many of the limitations inherent in traditional monolithic systems. Through isolating failures, encouraging redundancy, and supporting independent service deployment, they lay the groundwork for software environments that are agile and robust enough to meet modern demands.

Failure Mode Analysis Matrix

Service	Impact Level	Fallback Strategy	Recovery Time
Payment	Critical	Cache last status	< 30s
Inventory	High	Static backup	< 1m
Analytics	Low	Queue requests	< 5m
Logging	Medium	Local buffer	< 2m

Service Discovery and Auto-Scaling in Kubernetes

With microservices, efficient management helps sustain a system that performs well during varying loads and client demands. A critical component comes from effective service discovery. Service discovery in microservices lets client applications dynamically locate and connect to various services without manual intervention or hardcoded addresses. This dynamic aspect functions when services scale up or down or during deployments when new services start.

Kubernetes, the leading orchestration platform, brings built-in support for service discovery through its DNS-based solution, which seamlessly updates service information reflecting real-time cluster changes. This automation means developers don't have to worry about manually updating configuration files as the system evolves, making it incredibly efficient for scaling large applications. With Kubernetes, once you've set up your services and pods, everything just finds its place—almost like magic.

Service Configuration Matrix

Component	Purpose	Configuration	Scaling Trigger
DNS	Service discovery	ClusterIP	Load-based
Load Balancer	Traffic distribution	NodePort	Request count
Ingress	External access	LoadBalancer	TLS connections
Service Mesh	Communication	Internal	Latency

Practical Exercise: Kubernetes Setup

Configure service discovery:

- Service Definition

    ○ service name:

    ○ port mapping:

    ○ service type:

    ○ labels/selectors:

- DNS Configuration

    - domain pattern:

    - resolution policy:

    - TTL settings:

- Testing Plan

    - connectivity tests:

    - failover scenarios:

    - performance benchmarks:

Load Balancing and Resource Optimization

Service discovery in Kubernetes naturally integrates with load-balancing capabilities. When multiple replicas of a service exist, Kubernetes automatically distributes incoming traffic across these replicas. This built-in load-balancing allows for optimal resource utilization and maintains consistent performance across the cluster. The platform's service discovery mechanism continuously updates the load balancer with the latest service endpoint information, ensuring traffic is always directed to healthy instances.

Implementing Auto-Scaling

Now, while service discovery helps in connecting services, managing these connections dynamically requires an intelligent response to workload variations. Here's where Kubernetes' Horizontal Pod Autoscaler (HPA) steps in. HPA is a powerful feature that automatically scales the number of pods in a replication controller, deployment, or replica set based on observed CPU utilization or any other metric you choose. When you do this, HPA ensures that the application has enough resources to meet demand without overprovisioning infrastructure, which optimizes cost efficiency.

Consider how this plays out in a typical application scenario where traffic spikes due to seasonal sales events or promotional campaigns. HPA evaluates metrics like CPU usage and adjusts the number of running pods according to the current load, creating optimal performance. This automatic adjustment helps maintain the user experience consistently, regardless of fluctuating demand. Manual scaling would require constant monitoring and proactive anticipation of load changes, something not feasible at scale.

Proactive Scaling Strategies

Creating proactive scaling needs predictive scaling policies based on historical patterns and anticipated demand. This method prepares systems to handle known traffic spikes before they occur, preventing potential performance degradation. Teams should configure scaling rules that match regular patterns like daily peaks, weekly cycles, or seasonal variations, making resources available when needed.

Scaling Policy Template

- HPA Configuration:

  - resource metrics

  - CPU threshold (%):

  - memory threshold (%):

  - custom metrics:

- Scaling Rules

  - min replicas:

  - max replicas:

  - scale-up rate:

  - scale-down rate:

- Cooldown Periods

- Scale-up cooldown(s):

- Scale-down cooldown(s):

Load Testing Scenarios

Scenario	Load Pattern	Expected Scale	Recovery Time
Daily Peak	Gradual Increase	2x	5 min
Flash Sale	Sudden spike	5x	2 min
Background Jobs	Periodic	1.5x	10 min
Data Processing	Batch loads	3x	15 min

Exercise: Auto-Scaling Strategy

Design scaling rules:

- Service Analysis

    - Base load

    - Peak patterns

    - Resource usage

- Scale Triggers

    - Primary metric

    - Secondary metrics

    - Custom indicators

- Testing Approach

    - Load test scenarios

    - Performance targets

○ Validation criteria

Integrating Metrics and Monitoring

To make informed decisions about auto-scaling, it's crucial to integrate reliable metrics. Tools like Prometheus are important here, providing detailed insights into application performance. These metrics inform HPA about the real-time status of your services, enabling responsive scaling actions. For instance, if Prometheus detects increased CPU usage across multiple pods, HPA can trigger additional instances to handle the load efficiently, preventing potential downtime or performance degradation.

Monitoring and Alert Systems

Building comprehensive monitoring systems exceeds basic metrics collection. Teams should set up alerting mechanisms that detect and notify about anomalous behavior patterns. The alerts should follow appropriate thresholds that balance between being too sensitive and too lax. Integration with incident management systems lets teams respond quickly to scaling-related issues before they impact end users.

Monitoring Dashboard Layout

Metric Category	Key Metrics	Warning Threshold	Critical Threshold
Service Health	Uptime, Error Rate	95%, 1%	90%, 5%
Performance	Latency, Throughput	200ms, -10%	500 ms, -25%
Resources	CPU, Memory	70%, 80%	85%, 90%
Scaling	Pod Count, Queue Length	80%, 100	90%, 1000

Best Practices for Configuration

However, it's not just about having the tools but configuring them appropriately to respond to real-world scenarios. Best practices for setting up these configurations include rigorous testing of scaling policies under simulated loads. When creating test environments replicating possible high-demand situations, teams can observe how their scaling mechanisms react. This helps detect weaknesses or oversights before they impact production systems.

Proper documentation of the architecture and scaling strategies supports reliable setups. Clear documentation helps teams easily understand the rationale behind certain configurations and make necessary adjustments. This creates smoother knowledge transfer between teams, helping new members understand past decisions and future directions.

Service Definitions and Performance Benchmarks

Establishing clear service definitions includes defining resource requirements, scaling thresholds, and performance expectations for each service. These definitions should be accompanied by performance benchmarks that set baseline expectations for service behavior under different load conditions. Regular review and updates of these benchmarks ensure they remain relevant as the system evolves.

Operational Exercise

Create Operational Procedures:

- Incident Response

    - detection methods

    - response steps

    - escalation path

- Regular Maintenance

    - health checks

    - update strategy

    - backup procedures

- Documentation

- Architecture diagrams

- Runbooks

- Recovery procedures

Key Takeaway

- Microservices architecture improves system scalability and resilience by breaking applications into smaller, independent components that can operate independently, enhancing fault tolerance.

- Implementation of protective patterns like circuit breakers and fallback strategies ensures system robustness while maintaining service continuity during component failures.

- Kubernetes plays a crucial role in microservices operations by managing service discovery and auto-scaling, helping systems adapt to changing demands.

Chapter 10

Performance Monitoring and Tuning—Keep It Fast

D ata pipeline speed and efficiency depend on monitoring and tuning. As an engineer or developer who wants to learn how to keep systems running smoothly, you must master these concepts. Real-time monitoring identifies issues early and keeps our data moving uninterrupted. Using powerful tools like Prometheus and Grafana helps you keep an eye on performance and fine-tune processes for optimal efficiency. These tools reveal insights into data metrics and system health, creating a proactive defense against potential problems.

Here, you will

- understand how to integrate Prometheus for robust real-time monitoring and metric collection in data pipelines.

- master data visualization techniques using Grafana to create informative, actionable dashboards.

- learn effective strategies for managing data retention and storage optimization.

- develop skills in integrating monitoring systems within CI/CD pipelines for enhanced operational efficiency.

Setting Up Monitoring Systems With Prometheus and Grafana

Real-time monitoring helps data pipelines run optimally. Prometheus and Grafana are powerful tools that help manage performance. When integrated into existing systems, these tools reveal insights previously hidden, letting you stay ahead of potential issues.

Introduction to Prometheus

Let's start with Prometheus. It's a leading open-source system used for monitoring and alerting. What makes Prometheus stand out is its seamless integration with various data processing frameworks. Whether you're working with Apache Kafka, Spark, or Hadoop, Prometheus can gather important metrics without much hassle. This feature simplifies the metric collection process and allows for all necessary data to be captured in real time. What's good about Prometheus is its ability to scrape metrics from applications at specified intervals. When actively pulling this data, it becomes possible to store and analyze it for any anomalies or trends indicative of underlying performance issues.

Dimensional Data Model

Prometheus's dimensional data model sets it apart from traditional monitoring systems. Each metric is identified by its name and a set of key-value pairs called labels. This approach enables powerful querying capabilities through PromQL (Prometheus Query Language). For example, a single metric like "http_requests_total" can be tagged with labels such as "endpoint," "status_code," and "method," allowing you to analyze traffic patterns with incredible granularity. This multidimensional approach makes it possible to answer complex questions like 'What's the rate of 500 errors on the authentication endpoint for POST requests?' with a single query.

Alerting Capabilities

Prometheus's alerting system operates through AlertManager, which handles alert routing, grouping, and notification delivery. You can define alerting rules using PromQL expressions that specify conditions for triggering alerts.

Setting up Grafana

However, collecting metrics is just one part of the game. Visualization is where Grafana shines. Grafana connects directly with Prometheus, transforming raw data into comprehensive, visual dashboards. Imagine having a dashboard that showcases CPU usage spikes, memory consumption patterns, or network bottlenecks all in one place. This capability to create dynamic and interactive dashboards allows technical teams to grasp complex data quickly, making it easier to diagnose and resolve performance-related issues. Grafana isn't just about viewing data; it's about making informed decisions and being able to act on them promptly.

Alert Configuration

Grafana extends Prometheus's alerting capabilities with its visual alert configuration interface. Setting up alerts in Grafana involves defining evaluation criteria and notification channels:

1. Threshold-based alerts:

   ○ CPU Usage > 80% for 5 minutes

   ○ memory consumption exceeding 90% of allocated resources

   ○ latency spikes above 1000ms

2. Trend-based alerts:

   ○ sudden drops in throughput (>30% decrease)

   ○ gradual increase in error rates

   ○ anomaly detection based on historical patterns

Visualization Best Practices

When creating dashboards for data processing metrics, follow these visualization guidelines:

1. Group-related metrics: Combine CPU, memory, and disk metrics for each processing node.

2. Use appropriate visualization types

- line graphs for time-series data like throughput

- heatmaps for latency distribution

- gauges for current resource utilization

- tables for top-N queries

3. Implement consistent color coding

- red for errors/critical states

- yellow for warnings

- green for healthy states

Configuration Best Practices

Storage management shapes the success of monitoring. Collecting extensive data matters, but you must balance historical data retention against storage limitations. Retention policies solve this challenge. These policies set how long data stays. Setting retention periods based on data priority prevents unnecessary data accumulation while preserving valuable historical information. This strategy reduces database clutter and lowers storage costs.

Metric Collection Best Practices

To optimize metric collection while maintaining system performance:

1. Choose appropriate scrape intervals

- 15–30 seconds for standard metrics

- 5 seconds for critical performance metrics

- 1 minute for less critical, resource-intensive metrics

2. Implement efficient metric cardinality

- avoid high-cardinality labels

  ○ use recording rules for frequently used queries

  ○ set up job-specific scrape configs

3. Configure target discovery

  ○ use service discovery mechanisms

  ○ implement proper relabeling rules

  ○ set up federation for large-scale deployments

Security Configurations

Secure your monitoring infrastructure with these essential configurations:

1. Authentication

  ○ enable TLS for all connections

  ○ implement token-based authentication

  ○ use OAuth2 for Grafana login

2. Authorization

  ○ configure role-based access control (RBAC)

  ○ implement team-based dashboard access

  ○ set up read-only viewers for general users

3. Network Security

  ○ place Prometheus behind a reverse proxy

  ○ restrict access to AlertManager API

  ○ regular security audits and updates

Integrating Monitoring Into CI/CD

In real-time monitoring systems, integrating with Continuous Integration/Continuous Deployment (CI/CD) pipelines boosts DevOps speed. Connecting monitoring systems like Prometheus and Grafana with CI/CD pipelines sends alerts in real time. When you roll out code changes, you receive notifications if updates affect performance metrics. This setup delivers immediate feedback, supporting fast fixes. This creates a safety net, catching potential problems and maintaining your services smoothly.

Enhanced Feedback Loops

Strengthen your feedback loops by

1. Implementing Progressive Deployments

    o monitor key metrics during canary releases

    o set up automatic rollbacks based on error rates

    o compare performance metrics between versions

2. Creating Deployment-Specific Dashboards

    o real-time deployment status

    o before/after performance comparisons

    o impact analysis on dependent services

Implementation Guidelines

Setting up monitoring systems with Prometheus and Grafana follows clear steps. Start by defining metrics important to your specific application. Consider latency, throughput, and error rates. Then configure Prometheus to scrape these metrics from relevant endpoints. Next, link Prometheus to Grafana to create dashboards that show your system status. Last, integrate this monitoring setup into your CI/CD pipeline to automate finding and reporting performance issues.

Automated Tuning for Resolving Bottlenecks

For data systems, maintaining optimal throughput and efficiency matters most. Automated performance tuning fixes bottlenecks and maintains these systems smoothly.

Identifying Bottlenecks

One key strategy focuses on spotting bottleneck patterns like data skew and resource contention. Catching these patterns early, data engineers implement targeted solutions. Data skew happens as distribution becomes uneven across parallel processing units, forcing some units to work overloaded while others stay underutilized. Resource contention emerges as multiple processes compete over the same computational resources, causing delays and reducing system performance. Finding these issues quickly triggers strategic adjustments that balance resource allocation and stabilize data flow.

Monitoring Data Analysis

Understanding monitoring data requires a systematic approach to metrics collection and analysis. Key areas to monitor include:

System-Level Metrics

- CPU utilization across nodes

- memory consumption patterns

- network throughput and latency

- disk I/O performance

Application-Level Metrics

- query response times

- processing queue lengths

- thread pool utilization

- cache hit/miss ratios

Performance Diagnostic Tools

Modern tracing tools provide deep insights into system performance:

Distributed Tracing

- end-to-end request tracking

- service dependency mapping

- latency breakdown analysis

Profiling Tools

- hot spot identification

- memory leak detection

- thread contention analysis

Practice Exercises

Bottleneck Analysis

- Examine system metrics from a provided dataset and identify potential bottlenecks.

- Create a troubleshooting decision tree for common performance issues.

- Design a monitoring dashboard that highlights key performance indicators.

Case Studies

- Analyze a scenario where data skew caused processing delays.

- Review a real-world example of resource contention resolution.

- Develop an action plan for addressing identified bottlenecks.

Performance Benchmarking

Establishing performance baselines is another important component of ongoing tuning efforts. These baselines provide a reference point that represents normal operating conditions, allowing deviations to be easily spotted. As workload demands shift, comparing current performance against established baselines helps identify when and how to adjust system configurations or allocate additional resources.

Metric Category	Key Performance Indicators	Normal Range	Warning Threshold	Critical Threshold
Processing Speed	Records processed per second	800–1200	<800	<500
Response Time	Average query latency (ms)	100–300	>300	>500
Resource Usage	CPU utilization (%)	40–70	>70	>90
Memory	Heap usage (%)	60–80	>80	>90
Throughput	Transactions per minute	1000–1500	<1000	<800

Seasonal Pattern Analysis

Time-Based Patterns

- daily peaks and valleys

- weekly processing cycles

- monthly reporting impacts

- quarterly business events

- annual peak periods

Business-Driven Variations

- marketing campaign effects

- product launch impacts

- geographic usage patterns

- industry-specific cycles

- customer behavior trends

This proactive approach ensures that the system remains responsive to varying loads without requiring constant manual oversight. For instance, if a sudden spike in user activity surpasses the baseline, automated scripts might trigger scaling actions to manage the increased load.

Leveraging Automation Tools

Leveraging machine learning-driven tools can take performance optimization to the next level. These tools offer adaptive solutions by analyzing vast datasets to predict future performance trends and suggest changes. Machine learning algorithms can identify subtle patterns and correlations that might be missed by traditional methods. When integrating such tools into the system, data engineers can significantly reduce manual tuning efforts while achieving more precise outcomes. Say, a ML model might predict an impending resource bottleneck and recommend specific configuration changes that gradually adapt as new data becomes available, thereby maintaining system efficiency with minimal human intervention.

Tool Category	Primary Function	Use Cases	Implementation Complexity	ROI Timeline
Predictive Analytics	Performance forecasting	Capacity planning, Resource allocation	High	3–6 months
Auto-scaling	Dynamic resource management	Load balancing, Cost optimization	Medium	1–3 months
Configuration Tuning	Parameter optimization	Database settings, Application config	Medium-High	2–4 months
Anomaly Detection	Issue identification	Security, Performance monitoring	High	3–5 months
Self-healing Systems	Automated recovery	Error handling, Failover	Very High	6–12 months

Implementation Strategies

Phased Deployment

- initial monitoring phase

- controlled testing period

- gradual automation rollout

- full system integration

- continuous refinement

Risk Management

- fallback procedures

- performance impact assessment

- security considerations

- data privacy compliance

- change management protocols

Feedback Loops for Continuous Improvement

Continuous feedback loops from past adjustments further improve a culture of iterative performance improvement. Each modification provides valuable insights into what works and what needs refinement, creating a cycle of learning and adaptation. Feedback mechanisms can be implemented to collect data pre- and post-adjustment, offering a clear view of each change's impact. Over time, this feedback enriches the understanding of system behavior under different conditions and informs future tuning decisions. When you continually refine strategies based on empirical evidence, data systems becomes more resilient and capable of handling evolving demands.

Component	Data Sources	Collection Frequency	Action Triggers	Review Cycle
Performance Metrics	System logs, Monitoring tools	Real-time	Threshold violations	Daily
User Experience	Surveys, Support tickets	Weekly	Satisfaction drops	Monthly

System Changes	Change logs, Deployment records	Per event	Failed changes	Weekly
Resource Usage	Infrastructure metrics	Hourly	Capacity limits	Weekly
Incident Reports	Alert history, Post-mortems	Per incident	Pattern detection	Monthly

Integrating Strategies

Integrating these strategies into current operations requires deliberate planning and execution. Setting up automated monitoring systems, for instance, forms the foundation for recognizing bottleneck patterns. Such systems can continuously track key metrics like throughput, latency, and resource usage, alerting teams when anomalies arise. Also, using data visualization tools helps present complex information in an accessible manner, aiding in quick decision-making. Dashboards, for example, can display real-time data analytics, highlighting areas requiring attention and enabling teams to address issues promptly before they escalate.

Integrating ML Models

Incorporating ML models specifically designed for performance prediction and tuning is a practical step forward. These models can be trained on historical data to recognize normal patterns and anticipate deviations. When integrated into the operational workflow, they facilitate dynamic adjustments that optimize system performance without disrupting normal operations. A predictive model might forecast increased demand during peak hours and preemptively allocate resources, thus preventing potential slowdowns or outages.

Feedback Mechanisms

Establishing a feedback mechanism that captures detailed information about every adjustment contributes to building a knowledge base that guides future optimizations. This database might include records of the conditions that triggered changes, the specific actions taken, and their outcomes. When analyzing patterns within this data, organizations can identify best practices, refine automated responses, and develop a richer understanding of effective tuning approaches.

Ultimately, automating performance tuning to effectively resolve bottlenecks and maintain optimal throughput hinges on embracing a holistic approach that combines recognition, baselines, machine learning, and continuous feedback. These interwoven strategies not only streamline operations but also empower data engineers and developers to focus on innovation rather than firefighting issues. As workloads grow increasingly diverse and complex, maintaining a flexible yet robust tuning framework will be essential in navigating the challenges of modern data environments.

Key Takeaway

- Effective data pipeline maintenance relies on robust monitoring systems, with tools like Prometheus and Grafana providing valuable visualization and predictive insights.

- The combination of monitoring tools helps identify trends and potential issues early, enabling proactive problem-solving rather than reactive fixes.

- Automation of performance tuning processes, enhanced by machine learning capabilities, creates a dynamic system that can adapt to changing conditions.

Chapter 11

Real-World Case Studies—From Problem to Solution in Hours

Managing large-scale data challenges requires innovation, and companies like Netflix excel at this. When user experience shapes success or failure, Netflix's recommendation engine shows how smart data usage improves user engagement. Netflix processes vast amounts of data and turns this data into actionable insights that keep viewers coming back for more. When users open their Netflix account, they see a carefully curated list of shows and movies personally handpicked. That's not magic—it's the triumph of data engineering and analytical prowess, fine-tuned through continuous experimentation and effective architectural choices.

Here, you will learn:

- How Netflix transforms massive amounts of user interaction data into personalized recommendations through their sophisticated data processing pipeline and machine learning algorithms.

- The principles behind Netflix's microservices architecture and how it enables rapid innovation, independent scaling, and resilient operations across their global platform.

- Real-time data processing techniques using Apache Kafka and similar tools enable Netflix to provide instantaneous personalization and content delivery.

- Cloud-based strategies for handling massive scale and traffic surges, including Netflix's approach to regional failover and content delivery optimization.

- Architectural patterns and best practices for building highly available, scalable data systems inspired by Netflix's proven solutions in production.

Netflix's Recommendation Engine Architecture

Netflix's approach to real-time data processing demonstrates how to create tailored user experiences through its recommendation engine. This engine uses sophisticated personalization strategies to analyze vast amounts of user behavior data and create highly customized content suggestions. The algorithms analyze viewing habits, search histories, time spent on various genres, and metadata from viewed shows and predict what a user might want to watch next. When you open Netflix, it displays a lineup of titles based on careful data analysis, optimizing your streaming experience.

Key Components of Netflix's Data Architecture

Component	Purpose	Impact
Recommendation Engine	User Personalization	Enhanced Engagement
Microservices	Service Independence	Improved Scalability
Real-time Analytics	Continuous Learning	Dynamic Adoption
Cloud Infrastructure	Resource Management	Consistent Performance

Exercise: Recommendation System Design Challenge

You are tasked with designing a basic recommendation system, so consider:

1. What user data would you collect?

2. How would you prioritize different types of user interactions?

3. How would you handle cold starts for new users?

4. What metrics would you use to measure success?

Real-Time Analytics and Continuous Learning

The recommendation engine's power lies in its ability to process and analyze data in real-time. As users interact with the platform, their behaviors are instantly captured and processed, allowing the system to adapt recommendations dynamically. The continuous learning mechanism allows for the engine to evolve with user preferences, becoming more accurate over time. This real-time processing capability allows Netflix to handle billions of ratings daily, continuously refining its understanding of user preferences.

A/B Testing Framework

Netflix tests recommendation effectiveness through its A/B testing framework. Through methodical experiments, Netflix tests small changes on a subset of users before rolling them out to everyone. Changes include modifying thumbnail images or adjusting the order of suggested titles. They validate which changes improve user engagement and satisfaction. Through systematic experimentation, Netflix updates its interface and functionalities, making every adjustment improve the overall viewer experience without disrupting the browsing process.

A/B Testing Planning Framework

- Test Objective

    - primary metric

    - secondary metrics

- Test Parameters

    - control group size

    - test duration

○ success criteria

- Risk Assessment

    ○ potential user impact

    ○ fallback plan

Implementation Checklist

- baseline metrics gathered

- test groups defined

- monitoring setup

- success criteria established

Statistical Significance and Iterative Improvement

Netflix employs rigorous statistical significance testing to evaluate the results of their A/B tests. Each experiment is carefully designed with control groups and test groups to ensure reliable results. The iterative nature of their testing approach means that algorithms are constantly being refined based on experimental outcomes. This methodical process helps Netflix make data-driven decisions about which changes to implement at scale.

Case Study Exercise

Netflix-Style A/B Test Analysis

Given these hypothetical test results

- control group: 100,000 users

- test group: 100,000 users

- metric: Average viewing time

Questions

1. What sample size would you need for statistical significance?

2. How would you account for seasonal variations?

3. What secondary metrics would you monitor?

Microservices Architecture

The backbone supporting these efforts is Netflix's microservices architecture. Unlike traditional monolithic systems, microservices break down applications into smaller, independent units that handle specific tasks. For Netflix, this modularity means different parts of its platform—such as billing, user profiles, content browsing, and streaming—can evolve independently. They can scale services up or down based on demand, push updates without major disruptions, and reduce latency by optimizing each service individually. This independence allows Netflix to respond swiftly to changes in user demand and technological advancements, keeping their operations agile and efficient.

Microservices Implementation Checklist

- Service Boundaries Defined

- Communication Patterns Established

- Data Management Strategy

- Deployment Pipeline

- Monitoring Setup

- Error Handling

- Service Discovery

- Load Balancing

Inter-Service Communication and Development Cycles

The microservices architecture presents unique challenges in managing inter-service communication. Netflix has developed sophisticated service discovery and load-balancing mechanisms to allow efficient communication between services while minimizing latency.

This architecture also supports rapid development cycles, allowing teams to deploy updates to individual services without affecting the entire system. The result is a more resilient and maintainable platform that can evolve quickly while maintaining high availability.

Data Infrastructure

Let's examine the data infrastructure powering these operations. Netflix uses Apache Kafka to stream data and process and analyze it in real time. Apache Kafka functions as a data transport system, moving massive quantities of information with low latency, letting user interactions and feedback influence content recommendations almost instantaneously. This matters most during peak times when millions of viewers log on simultaneously, needing smooth service and accurate suggestions.

Netflix utilizes a cloud-based solution to maintain elasticity during demand surges, such as when a new season of a hit show is released or during global lockdowns. Cloud solutions offer the flexibility to scale resources dynamically, accommodating fluctuating traffic without sacrificing performance. The system helps Netflix prevent outages or slowdowns during critical viewing periods and maintains high-quality streaming for millions of global viewers.

At the core of these technological feats is a commitment to continuous improvement and adaptation. Netflix's ability to harness advanced data processing techniques to boost viewer satisfaction exemplifies how companies can tackle complex data challenges and turn them into opportunities for growth and innovation. Their strategic use of personalized recommendations, robust testing frameworks, flexible architectures, and dynamic data infrastructures serves as a model for other data-intensive applications striving to deliver exceptional user experiences.

Amazon's Handling of Flash Sales and Traffic Spikes

When it comes to handling the incredible influx of users during flash sales, Amazon has honed its strategies into a formidable model of scalable architecture. At the heart of this approach is event-driven architecture, a system designed to react automatically when certain events occur. Imagine this: During a flash sale, thousands upon thousands of customers flood the site. An event-driven architecture allows Amazon's systems to sense these spikes in activity and scale accordingly, triggering additional resources on demand. This means that the company isn't over-preparing with excessive resources at all times; instead, they have the flexibility to upscale operations only when necessary. This smart approach saves costs and improves the user experience by reducing wait times and ensuring smooth transactions.

Real-Time Data Streaming and Event Sourcing

The architecture's power lies in its sophisticated real-time data streaming capabilities, processing millions of concurrent events without delay. Event sourcing plays an important role by capturing every user interaction as an immutable event, creating a comprehensive audit trail for analytics. This approach not only helps in understanding user behavior patterns but also enables the system to replay events for testing and debugging purposes.

Dynamic Resource Allocation

Now picture Amazon's strategy as not just reactive but highly dynamic. Dynamic resource allocation plays a key role here. It involves using auto-scaling groups that continuously monitor performance and traffic levels. For example, if a product goes viral thanks to a flash sale, the infrastructure can increase server capacity seamlessly to accommodate the sudden rush of visitors. When implementing such intelligent resource management strategies, Amazon allows continuous availability without degrading service quality. Users can browse, select, and purchase without facing the dreaded spinning wheel of loading screens—a nightmare scenario during high-demand periods.

Cloud Services Integration

Amazon's infrastructure uses advanced cloud services integration, providing seamless resource scaling across multiple availability zones. They implement sophisticated load-balancing strategies for high availability during extreme traffic spikes. The system automatically provisions new resources in different geographical locations for optimal performance across global regions.

Caching Mechanisms

Another cornerstone of managing high traffic effectively is caching mechanisms. Technologies such as Memcached or Redis are critical in handling data requests quickly. These caching solutions store frequently accessed information closer to the user, reducing the time it takes to fetch data from back-end services every time it's needed. Think of it like having a super-efficient library where the most popular books are kept right at the entrance for easy access. This practice lightens the load on Amazon's main servers, maintaining performance integrity even when demand skyrockets.

Cache Invalidation Strategies

Protecting data integrity while caching matters. Amazon implements sophisticated cache invalidation strategies, so users see the most current information. This includes time-based expiration for volatile data, event-based invalidation for immediate updates, and versioning mechanisms for managing concurrent modifications. These strategies mean caching improves performance without compromising data accuracy.

Flash Sale System Design

Scenario: Design a system to handle Black Friday sale traffic—

Requirements

- 1 million concurrent users

- 100,000 transactions per minute

- 99.99% uptime

Tasks

1. Outline your caching strategy.

2. Design your auto-scaling rules.

3. Plan your monitoring approach.

4. Define your failure scenarios and recovery plans.

Monitoring and Real-Time Analytics

But what keeps this whole operation running smoothly is real-time monitoring and analytics. During flash sales, tools and KPIs are employed to keep tabs on potential bottlenecks. It's like having a control room with eyes everywhere—monitoring server loads, user pathways, and transaction speeds. When the system detects any slowdown or strain, immediate adjustments are made to redistribute traffic, reallocate resources, or resolve issues before they escalate. It's this proactive stance that keeps everything ticking nicely during a peak rush.

In practical terms, this means that Amazon leverages a mix of sophisticated software and timely human intervention. Engineers and developers work with advanced analytical tools to interpret data in real time. They can spot trends or anomalies and act swiftly—almost like digital firefighters putting out sparks before they become fires. This capability is important because even a slight hitch can lead to significant lost revenue and customer dissatisfaction in the fast-paced world of e-commerce.

Also, by constantly refining their KPIs and analytical models, Amazon iterates on past experiences to improve future responses. Each flash sale becomes a learning opportunity, honing the system further to anticipate and manage high-traffic scenarios more efficiently. This iterative improvement reflects an understanding that technology is ever-evolving and that staying ahead requires continual adaptation.

Critical Monitoring Metrics

Metric Category	Key Metrics	Alert Threshold
System Health	CPU, Memory, Disk	80% utilization
User Experience	Response Time, Error Rate	>2s, >0.1%
Business Impact	Transaction Rate, Success Rate	<95% baseline

Performance Monitoring Tools

Amazon employs a comprehensive suite of monitoring tools that track various performance metrics. These tools provide detailed insights into system health, including response times, error rates, resource utilization, and user experience metrics. The monitoring system uses ML algorithms to detect anomalies and predict potential issues before they impact users, allowing proactive problem resolution.

These methodologies collectively form the robust backbone of Amazon's ability to handle massive amounts of traffic effortlessly. And while these techniques sound advanced, they're rooted in principles that many data engineers and technical professionals can apply to their projects. Thinking about scaling not as a static challenge but as a dynamic, responsive task is relevant. It's about designing systems that don't just meet today's needs but are also prepared to evolve alongside growing demands.

Chapter Review Exercise

Apply the lessons from Netflix and Amazon to design a high-scale system:

1. Choose between a video streaming service or e-commerce platform

2. Outline your

    a. core services

    b. data flow

    c. scaling strategy

    d. monitoring approach

3. Explain how your design handles

    a. traffic spikes

    b. data processing

    c. user experience

d. system reliability

Final Insights

- Netflix and Amazon demonstrate successful large-scale data management through different approaches: Netflix focuses on personalization through recommendation engines and A/B testing, while Amazon excels at handling sudden traffic spikes through event-driven architecture.

- Both companies leverage microservices architecture effectively: Netflix for independent service adaptation and Amazon for dynamic resource allocation during high-traffic events like flash sales.

- Advanced caching strategies and real-time analytics play crucial roles in maintaining performance under heavy loads, with both companies implementing sophisticated monitoring systems to prevent issues.

Chapter 12

Building Your Own Portfolio of Scalable Systems

Creating scalable systems shows your skills and establishes yourself as a distinguished candidate in the data engineering field. A tangible collection of projects that displays your ability to design and implement efficient, reliable data pipelines strengthens your professional appeal. Beyond listing technical abilities on a resume, you need concrete evidence of your capacity to tackle complex problems with real-world applications. A compelling project portfolio proves your readiness and capability to handle the demands of modern data-intensive environments.

Below, we will discuss

- how to select and develop compelling data engineering projects that demonstrate essential skills like ETL pipeline creation, real-time data processing, and scalable system design.

- the fundamentals of building a microservices-based portfolio project that showcases your understanding of modern distributed system architectures.

- Best practices for implementing and documenting data lake solutions, demonstrating your ability to handle large-scale data storage and management challenges.

- strategies for effectively documenting your projects, including technical decisions, problem-solving approaches, and performance optimizations that highlight your professional thought process.

- techniques for structuring your portfolio to showcase both breadth of knowledge and depth of expertise in key data engineering competencies.

Highlights of Valuable Projects for Job Market Appeal

For showcasing your skills in data engineering, a strong portfolio contains projects that make a tangible impact. Real-time streaming data projects display technical prowess and the ability to bring data to life through visualization. The speed at which data is processed and insights emerge, creates a difference. Consider building a dashboard that streams live analytics for social media sentiment or financial market trends. This displays your expertise in handling data velocity and variety and gives stakeholders immediate insights.

Technology Stack and Implementation

Building real-time data projects typically involves working with technologies like Apache Kafka for stream processing, real-time databases for storage, and modern visualization frameworks. The implementation should demonstrate proficiency in handling data streams, processing events in real-time, and creating intuitive visualizations that make complex data accessible to end-users. Understanding user experience principles in data applications is crucial for creating dashboards that effectively communicate insights.

Exercise: Design a Real-Time Analytics Dashboard

Scenario: Create a social media sentiment analysis dashboard:

Requirements

1. Handle 1000 tweets per second.

2. Calculate sentiment in real-time.

3. Update dashboard every 5 seconds.

4. Store historical data.

Questions to address

1. What technologies would you choose and why?

2. How would you handle data spikes?

3. What backup strategies would you implement?

Robust ETL Pipeline Projects

Creating a robust ETL pipeline is another quintessential project. This cornerstone of data engineering underscores your ability to manage large-scale data processing efficiently. It's not just about moving data from point A to point B; it's about making sure every step maintains data quality and integrity. Batch jobs must be orchestrated seamlessly to prevent bottlenecks and uphold reliability. For instance, developing an ETL system for a retail company might involve extracting sales data from multiple sources, transforming it into a consistent format, and loading it into a centralized platform for analysis. This showcases your expertise in synchronizing diverse datasets and delivering high-quality results, which are crucial traits that employers look for.

ETL Pipeline Design Matrix

Component	Technologies	Considerations	Monitoring
Extract	[Tools]	[Challenges]	[Metrics]
Transform	[Tools]	[Challenges]	[Metrics]
Load	[Tools]	[Challenges]	[Metrics]

Orchestration and Workflow Management

Demonstrating proficiency with workflow management tools like Apache Airflow or Luigi shows the ability to handle complex data pipelines. Implementation of error handling, retry mechanisms, and monitoring systems proves understanding of production-grade ETL requirements. Experience with data quality checks and validation procedures throughout the pipeline showcases attention to data integrity.

Microservices-Based ETL Architecture

Now, leveraging microservices architecture within your ETL design is where things start to get modular and exciting. In contrast to monolithic designs, microservices allow you to build applications as a suite of small services, each running its own process and communicating with lightweight mechanisms. This approach reflects a mastery of creating systems that are scalable, flexible, and easily maintainable. Picture designing an ETL pipeline where each transformation step is handled by separate microservices. It's like having specialized units, each performing a distinct task, improving the system's robustness. Such projects highlight your capability to work with cloud-native architectures—skills in high demand as organizations increasingly adopt cloud computing to build efficient, resilient systems.

Cloud-Native Implementation

Showing experience with container orchestration platforms like Kubernetes and service mesh technologies shows an understanding of modern microservices' deployment. The implementation of service discovery, load-balancing, and fault tolerance mechanisms proves capability in building resilient distributed systems.

Exercise: Microservices Architecture Design

Design a microservices-based data processing system that:

1. processes customer data

2. handles multiple data formats

3. scales automatically

4. maintains data consistency

Deliverables

- service boundary definitions

- communication patterns

- deployment strategy

- monitoring approach

Data Lake Implementation

Incorporating a data lake into your portfolio is yet another powerful demonstration of your competence. Data lakes are repositories for structured and unstructured data, allowing organizations to store vast amounts of information from various sources in their native formats. Setting up a data lake involves strategic decisions about storage solutions, data access methods, and governance practices, demonstrating holistic thinking about data management. Say you are creating a data lake solution for an e-commerce entity wherein customer behavior logs, transaction records, and inventory data reside cohesively. This would showcase not only your understanding of storage technologies and data accessibility but also your proficiency in ensuring data compliance and governance measures are in place.

These projects are more than bullet points on a resume—they're reflections of practical knowledge applied creatively to solve real-world problems. Real-time data processing projects highlight your ability to derive actionable insights swiftly, a critical advantage in making informed business decisions quickly. Solid ETL pipelines allow seamless flow of data across systems with attention to accuracy and efficiency, proving you can handle complex processes reliably. Adopting microservices underpins your fluency in contemporary software development, a methodology that enhances scalability and adaptability. Lastly, data lakes underline your strategic perspective on long-term data storage and governance, which are key aspects in today's data-driven environments.

While embarking on these projects, consider them as learning journeys. Each stage, from ideation to deployment, offers opportunities to refine your technical abilities and problem-solving skills. Real-time data projects push you to think on your feet and adapt to changing requirements. Building ETL systems teaches you discipline in data hygiene and resilience against system failures. Microservices architecture introduces a mindset shift towards thinking in terms of independent yet interrelated components. Creating a data lake unfolds complexities in balancing accessibility with security, a lesson in managing resources wisely.

Data Lake Planning Template

- Storage Zones

  - raw data zone

  - processed zone

  - curated zone

- Access Patterns

  - read patterns

  - write patterns

  - security levels

- Governance

  - metadata management

  - data catalog

  - access controls

Governance and Security Implementation

Showing implementation of data governance frameworks, including metadata management systems and data lineage tracking. Showcasing security measures such as access control mechanisms, encryption strategies, and compliance monitoring proves an understanding of enterprise-grade data lake requirements.

Guidance on Expanding Projects With More Complex Features

In building a portfolio of scalable systems, improving existing projects with sophisticated features increases their complexity and relevance. Consider adding predictive analytics to your data pipelines. This integrating machine learning adds value while showing your capability to derive actionable insights from data. With predictive analytics, you will work with various machine learning algorithms. Start with regression models or decision trees and explore advanced techniques like ensemble methods or neural networks. This creates a rich exploration of how different algorithms respond to your specific datasets, and when you're predicting customer behavior or optimizing logistics, your skills become invaluable.

Project Enhancement Checklist

Advanced Feature Implementation

- predictive analytics integration

- automated data validation

- real-time monitoring

- front-end visualization

- multicloud support

- security measures

- performance optimization

- documentation

Data Pipeline and Model Integration

The integration of ML models into data pipelines requires careful consideration of workflow orchestration. This includes establishing automated processes for model training, validation, and deployment. Understanding how to create efficient pipelines that handle both data preprocessing and model serving demonstrates advanced architectural thinking. Implementation should include version control for models, feature engineering pipelines, and model performance monitoring systems.

Exercise: Pipeline Enhancement Challenge

Given a basic ETL pipeline, design improvements for:

1. machine learning model integration

2. data quality validation

3. performance monitoring

4. error handling

5. scalability optimization

Portfolio Review Template
- Project Overview

    ○ business problem

    ○ technical solution

    ○ architecture diagram

- Implementation Details

    ○ technology stack

    ○ key challenges

    ○ solutions implemented

- Results and Metrics

    ○ performance data

    ○ scalability tests

    ○ lessons learned

Robust Data Validation Processes

After integrating ML, upgrading your projects with data validation processes improves reliability. Quality and accuracy stand as non-negotiable. Using tools and techniques for automating the monitoring of data feeds catches anomalies early. Use frameworks like Apache NiFi or Pachyderm to help automate data ingestion while tracking validation rules.

Then, alert systems with Amazon CloudWatch or Microsoft Azure Monitor can be configured for real-time notifications when data deviates from expected patterns. Following best practices strengthens your project and shows potential employers your focus on data integrity.

Advanced Monitoring and Logging

Implementation of comprehensive logging systems that track data lineage and quality metrics throughout the pipeline. Development of custom validation rules and data quality checks that enforce business rules and data consistency. Integration of anomaly detection systems that can identify and flag unusual patterns in data streams, demonstrating an understanding of data quality management at scale.

Front-End Development for Data Interaction

Consider building the front end for data interaction, which follows user experience design principles. Creating an intuitive and responsive user interface for data applications makes complex data accessible to non-technical users. Start by using modern web development frameworks like React or Angular to build dynamic interfaces that allow users to interact with data. Include visualization libraries like D3.js or Tableau to transform raw data into meaningful insights through charts and dashboards. This aspect displays your ability to bridge the gap between technical prowess and user-centric design, making your projects stand out.

Stakeholder Engagement Through Data

Developing interactive features that allow stakeholders to explore data through customizable visualizations and reports. Implementation of real-time updates and notifications to keep users informed of important changes or trends. Creating intuitive interfaces for data exploration that cater to different user roles and technical expertise levels.

Multicloud Infrastructure Support

Expanding your infrastructure scope by supporting multicloud deployments increases complexity in your portfolio. Companies choose cloud solutions, so skills in deploying applications across multiple cloud providers are valuable. Multicloud strategies offer vendor diversity, creating resilience and flexibility in your projects. They present challenges, particularly in cross-vendor data integration. Tools like Terraform or Kubernetes manage orchestration and integration across cloud environments like AWS, Google Cloud, and Azure. Learning these areas trains you for real-world scenarios where businesses use different cloud vendors.

Multicloud Infrastructure Management Tools

Tool	Primary Purpose	Cloud Providers Supported	Key Benefits	Challenges
Terraform	Infrastructure provisioning	AWS, GCP, Azure, Others	Version-controlled infrastructure, Declarative syntax	State management complexity
Kubernetes	Container orchestration	All major providers	Portable workloads, Auto-scaling	Complex setup and maintenance
Ansible	Configuration management	Any cloud or on-premise	Agentless, Simple syntax	Limited cloud-native features
CloudFormation	AWS resource management	AWS only	Deep AWS integration, Built-in validation	Vendor lock-in
Pulumi	Infrastructure as code	All major providers	Modern programming	Steeper learning curve

			languages, Strong typing	
Azure ARM	Azure resource management	Azure only	Native Azure integration, Role-based access	Limited to Azure ecosystem

Infrastructure as Code Practices

Implement infrastructure as code (IaC) through automated deployment pipelines across multiple cloud providers. Create modular and reusable infrastructure components adaptable to different cloud environments. Set up monitoring and cost optimization strategies for multicloud deployments to prove understanding of cloud resource management.

Key Takeaways

- A strong project portfolio is crucial for career advancement in data engineering, demonstrating practical skills through real-world applications like streaming projects, ETL pipelines, and microservices architecture.

- Each project serves dual purposes: Showcasing technical expertise while highlighting problem-solving abilities and creativity in transforming complex data challenges into practical solutions.

- Thorough documentation of the entire project lifecycle, from conception to deployment, creates compelling narratives for potential employers while tracking personal growth.

Conclusion

In this final section about data systems, we'll review all you've learned. You've made significant progress, converting abstract concepts into practical applications and providing you with skills to handle any data-intensive challenge. Remember Chapter 3, where you built your first real-time data pipeline—moving from theoretical understanding to practical implementation? You learned, discovering how to turn ideas into concrete results, with each chapter adding new technical capabilities.

In these chapters, we've covered important lessons necessary for anyone working with data at scale. The interplay of batch and real-time processing discussed in Chapter 4 shows how to determine when to use each to improve efficiency and performance in your systems. You learned about scalable microservices in Chapter 9, which teaches you how to create reliable systems that perform well under stressful conditions. You can apply these principles to your actual projects.

Continuous learning drives success in data systems. Data system technologies change rapidly, introducing new technologies and methodologies. You've learned current techniques and ways to adapt to future changes. Chapter 10 covers improving performance through monitoring. Keep pushing forward. Study new developments and test different approaches to stay competitive. When you're studying advancements in machine learning integrations or improving distributed systems, maintain your curiosity.

You've accomplished significant technical goals. You've grown from understanding theory to becoming someone who can build high-availability database systems. You've developed skills to solve complex problems, create solutions, and advance the industry. Build your portfolio of projects showing your growth into a practitioner who can build sophisticated solutions. Your projects demonstrate your dedication, hard work, and technical expertise.

The industry values skill and the ability to adapt and grow. Share your work; make your projects demonstrate your capabilities and problem-solving abilities. Join communities, share your insights, learn from others, and contribute to discussions about the future of data systems. Connect with and build a community of skilled individuals who create better solutions together.

Watch developing trends in the industry. Study advancements in real-time analytics, AI, and ML for predictive data analysis, data privacy, and ethical data handling. Technical professionals lead, predict shifts, and guide organizations through changes in data technology.

Remember, building proficiency in data engineering is a marathon, not a sprint. There's always something new to learn, another layer to uncover, and further depth to achieve. Let this book serve as both a foundation and a springboard, pushing you to delve deeper into areas that intrigue you. Perhaps it's improving your skills in data visualization or mastering new frameworks for even more effective processing—whatever your path, let it be driven by curiosity and the pleasure of discovery.

In closing, this book is more than just a guide—it's a companion on your professional journey. You've embarked upon a path filled with opportunities to make significant impacts, whether by streamlining processes within an organization or by innovating groundbreaking technologies. Celebrate each milestone, embrace every challenge as a chance to learn, and continue pushing the envelope in your work. The world of data offers endless possibilities, and with the skills and insights gained here, you're well-equipped to chart your own course. Remember, this is just the beginning. So, keep coding, keep experimenting, and most importantly, keep imagining what's possible. Your journey in data engineering is far from over—it's merely the start of an exciting adventure.

References

A complete guide to ETL pipeline for beginners. (2019). Rising Wave
https://risingwave.com/blog/a-complete-guide-to-etl-pipeline-for-beginners/

A comprehensive guide to microservices architecture: Benefits, challenges, and best practices. (2024). WebcluesInfotech. https://www.webcluesinfotech.com/a-comprehensive-guide-to-microservices-architecture-benefits-challenges-and-best-practices/

Abeykoon, V., & Fox, G. C. (2023, May 3). *Trends in high-performance data engineering for data analytics.* IntechOpen. https://www.intechopen.com/chapters/1136439

Alagar. (2023, September 28). The role of data engineering in real-time analytics. *IABAC.* https://iabac.org/blog/the-role-of-data-engineering-in-real-time-analytics

Best practices for achieving low latency in system design. (2024, September 10). *Educative.* https://www.educative.io/blog/low-latency-in-system-design

Building scalable data pipelines: Tools and techniques for modern data engineering. (2024a, August 29). GeeksforGeeks. https://www.geeksforgeeks.org/building-scalable-data-pipelines-tools-and-techniques-for-modern-data-engineering/

Database sharding: Concepts & examples. (n.d.). MongoDB. https://www.mongodb.com/resources/products/capabilities/database-sharding-explained

Egwom, O. J. (2023). Real-Time data processing in edge computing: Opportunities and challenges. ResearchGate. https://www.researchgate.net/publication/377980274_Real-Time_Data_Processing_in_Edge_Computing_Opportunities_and_Challenges

GaperNetflix's tech stack secrets: A closer look. (2023, November 1). Gaper.io. https://gaper.io/netflix-tech-stack-secrets/

How to build a data pipeline: A comprehensive guide. (2024, September 19). Rishabh Software. https://www.rishabhsoft.com/blog/how-to-build-a-data-pipeline

Jaffery, A. (2023, December 7). *Understanding ETL batch processing.* Astera. https://www.astera.com/type/blog/etl-batch-processing/

Jatin. (2023, September 13). *Mastering spark jobs: Comprehensive guide for data engineers.* Decube Inc. https://www.decube.io/post/spark-jobs-data-engineers-guide

Li, C., Chen, Y., & Shang, Y. (2022). A review of industrial big data for decision making in intelligent manufacturing. *ScienceDirect: Engineering Science and Technology, an International Journal, 29, 101021.* https://www.sciencedirect.com/science/article/pii/S2215098621001336

Modupe, O. T., Otitoola, A. A., Oladapo, O. J., Abiona, O. O., Oyeniran, O. C., Adewusi, A. O., Komolafe, A. M., & Obijuru, A. (2024). Reviewing the transformational impact of edge computing on real-time data processing and analytics. *Computer Science & IT Research Journal, 5*(3), 693–702. https://doi.org/10.51594/csitrj.v5i3.929

Nero, R. del. (2023, October 2). *Learn when to use database replica and database sharding for systems design.* Java Challengers. https://javachallengers.com/database-replica-and-sharding/

Smallcombe, M. (2024, February 15). *SQL vs nosql: 5 critical differences.* Integrate.io. https://www.integrate.io/blog/the-sql-vs-nosql-difference/

Sujatha, R. (2024). *Horizontal scaling vs vertical scaling: Choosing your strategy.* Digitalocean.com. https://www.digitalocean.com/resources/articles/horizontal-scaling-vs-vertical-scaling

WebSockets for realtime distributed systems. (2024b, September 26). GeeksforGeeks. https://www.geeksforgeeks.org/websockets-for-real-time-distributed-systems/

Wickramasinghe, S. (n.d.). SQL vs. nosql today: Databases, differences & when to use which. *Splunk-Blogs*. https://www.splunk.com/en_us/blog/learn/sql-vs-nosql.html

Book Description

Unleash the Power of Your Data

You've probably found yourself drowning in a sea of data, wondering how on earth you can make sense of all those numbers and trends. It's like trying to find a needle in a haystack, right? You're not just looking at a bunch of numbers; you're staring at insights that could drive your business forward or hold it back. Imagine transforming that data deluge into a streamlined process that makes your life easier and unlocks opportunities left and right.

This book isn't just another tech manual; it's your ticket to mastering data engineering in a way that's practical and relatable. We dive into hands-on projects that not only teach you the fundamentals but also empower you to build scalable, efficient systems.

Here's a taste of what you'll get:

- **Hands-on projects to put theory into practice.**

- **Techniques to optimize processing speed and efficiency.**

- **Insights into real-time data systems and how to leverage them.**

Don't just learn data engineering—experience it and transform your understanding into real-world applications that rock the data landscape!

Made in the USA
Coppell, TX
20 February 2025

46170139R00181